GENDER EQUITY IN EDUCATION

An Annotated Bibliography

Beverly A. Stitt

Southern Illinois University Press
Carbondale and Edwardsville

Printed in the United States of America
Edited by Jill Butler
Designed by Robyn Laur Clark
Production supervised by Natalia Nadraga
97 96 95 94   4 3 2 1

Library of Congress Cataloging-in-Publication Data

Stitt, Beverly A., 1943–
    Gender equity in education : an annotated bibliography / Beverly
A. Stitt.
    p.   cm.
    1. Sex discrimination in education—United States—Bibliography.
2. Sexism in education—United States—Bibliography. 3. Educational
equalization—United States. 4. Women—Education—United States—
Bibliography.
    Z5814.D5S75   1994
    [LC212.82]
    016.37019'345—dc20   93-24315
    ISBN 0-8093-1937-3   CIP

The paper used in this publication meets the minimum requirements of
American National Standard for Information Sciences—Permanence
of Paper for Printed Library Materials, ANSI Z39.48-1984. ♾

CONTENTS

PREFACE

This bibliography was begun in 1985 by staff of the Illinois Building Fairness Resource Center, which I directed and which was supported through the Illinois State Board of Education with funds originating from the Carl D. Perkins Vocational Education Act of 1984. One of the center's objectives was to provide suggestions of specific resources for use by administrators, teachers, and counselors in their attempts to overcome gender role stereotyping and sex bias in schools. After the close of the Building Fairness Resource Center, I continued adding to the bibliography through early 1993.

As I reviewed the hundreds of articles, curriculum guides, books, workshop guides, videos, and classroom activities pertaining to this subject, it became evident that not all materials with promising titles and subtitles lived up to their promises. I omitted outdated or poorly developed materials that use concepts or examples that might create more amusement than understanding of the equity issues. However, some materials developed as early as the 1970s or early 1980s remain useful, and I included them. Only those materials I deem worthy for use in the recommended settings are described in the annotations. Many of the materials included in the bibliography are available for loan or purchase. I provided ordering information where it was available to me, but because of possible price adjustments over time, I did not include cost information. I also included additional information for videotapes, filmstrips, and slide presentations where it was available to me.

Each entry appears once in the bibliography, under the most pertinent category. Entry codes are listed in the index under other relevant categories where appropriate. Readers may look up specific categories of interest to them in the index and locate the entry codes indicating the bibliographical categories in which resources are described. I hope that this bibliography will provide professional sex equity staff, administrators, teachers, and counselors with a reliable, easy to use guide for selecting materials and readings.

I gratefully acknowledge appreciation to Becky Markham, a resource specialist, Sandra Wagner, a marvel with the computer, and Julie Feig, Angie Bush, and Deb Morrow who tirelessly edited and revised entries.

GENDER
EQUITY IN
EDUCATION

1 Agriculture and Industry (AI)

AI1. *The Aerospace Career Handbook.* Anne Cardoze. New York: Arco Publishing, 1985.

> Describes a wide variety of jobs in the aerospace industry. Includes 155 pages of educational and training requirements. Discusses where the jobs are and will be in the future, and women in aerospace and technical communications.

AI2. *Analysis of Student, Parent, and Educator Barriers Preventing Female Participation in Wyoming Secondary School Industrial Education Courses.* Cameron K. Allen. Project report. Laramie, WY: University of Wyoming, 1983.

> Describes a Wyoming project to identify and define barriers to female enrollment in industrial education. Includes statistics on female enrollment in industrial education and recommendations for reduction or elimination of any barriers. Order from Department of Vocational Education, University of Wyoming, Laramie, WY 82070.

AI3. *Cowgirls.* Teresa Jordan. Santa Rosa, CA: National Women's History Project, 1984.

> Considers the experiences of cowgirls from the 1870s to the present from various points of view, including mother/daughter tradition, rancher's daughter, husband/wife team, women alone, women ranch hands, and women professional rodeo performers. Order from P.O. Box 3716, Santa Rosa, CA 95402.

AI4. *Cowgirls Coloring Book.* Ubet Tomb and Nancy Conkle. Santa Rosa, CA: National Women's History Project, 1985.

> Includes full-page pictures and smaller portraits of cowgirls and their horses, biographies, and more general articles. Text is for junior high and up; pictures are appropriate for any age. Order from P.O. Box 3716, Santa Rosa, CA 95402.

AI5. "The Lady Runs a Ranch." Roberta Donovan. *Sperry-New Holland News*, June/July 1984, 4–5.

Describes the satisfactions and skills of a nontraditional career. Presents a very positive picture of this career option for a female.

AI6. *Sex Equity Guide for Industrial Education Programs.* Pamphlet. Springfield, IL: Illinois State Board of Education, 1981.

Explains how industrial education may be beneficial to all students, regardless of sex, and gives 12 pages of strategies for achieving gender equity in industrial education. Order from 100 N. First St., Springfield, IL 62777.

AI7. "Women in Agricultural Education." *Agricultural Education Magazine*, Apr. 1987.

Devotes the entire issue to the concerns and issues of women in agricultural education.

AI8. "Women Probe Agriculture's Future." Lorraine Stuart Merrill. *Ford-New Holland News*, Jan./Feb. 1993, 4–18.

Contains six sketches of women working in various agricultural occupations, including researching alternatives to herbicides in corn, sustainable agriculture, and environmentally neutral food systems; prize cattle ranching; and establishing farm political organizations. Devotes entire issue to women's contributions to agriculture.

2

B1. *Clerical Work: A Manual for Change*. Report of the Permanent Commission on the Status of Women on Sex Discrimination in Clerical Work. Hartford, CT: Commission on the Status of Women, 1978.

> Includes a survey designed to assess the most significant problems faced by clerical workers; a series of interviews conducted with executives of major companies, representatives of unions, and personnel consultants to get their views on the actuality and possibility of upward mobility in clerical work; and a public hearing report where clerical workers gave personal testimony on the problems they faced on their jobs.

B2. "The Corporate Woman." *Wall Street Journal*, special report, 24 Mar. 1986, sec. 4.

> Includes a group of articles: "The Glass Ceiling" (why women cannot seem to break the invisible barrier that blocks them from the top jobs), "Venturing Out" (the small business alternative), "Room at the Top" (a progress report on women in industry), "The Board Game" (playing musical directors), "Following the Leaders" (the generation gap between pioneers and M.B.A.'s), "A Road Already Traveled" (a talk with Wharton women), "Reel-Life Struggles" (men and power in Hollywood), "The Industrial Revolution" (women running factories), "The New Majorities" (the pink-collar ghettos), "Prisoners of the Past" (marketers struggle with outmoded notions), "The Last Angry Men" (companies confront male backlash), "Gentlemen of the Club" (the all-male enclaves), "Clearer Connections" (new perspectives on old networks), "Strangers in a Strange Land" (African-American women adapting to management roles), "Family Practices" (maternal management in an aerospace firm), "My Lover, My Colleague" (office romance comes out of the closet), "Courting the Couple" (corporate approaches to the dual-career couple), "Scenes from Two Marriages" (juggling

two careers), "How to Do Everything Better" (a look at books for aspiring executives), and "The New Double Standard" (the changing rules of office etiquette).

B3.   *Corporate Women: A Critical Business Resource.* Pamphlet. New York: Catalyst, 1987.

> Maintains it is critical for businesses to continue to develop women for top positions. Order from 250 Park Ave. South, New York, NY 10003.

B4.   *Corporate Women's Groups: A Business Resource.* Pamphlet. New York: Catalyst, 1987.

> Discusses the benefits that corporate women's groups offer management and members. Order from 250 Park Ave. South, New York, NY 10003.

B5.   *Entrepreneurship for Women: Escape from the Pink-Collar Ghetto.* Charlotte Taylor. Videocassette. Columbus, OH: National Center on Research in Vocational Education, n.d.

> Addresses the movement of American women into small business ventures. The phenomenon is occurring because women more than ever before are recognizing the marketplace, rather than the work force, as a place they can live out their aspirations and be rewarded for their talents. For many, small business ownership has already become the way out of the pink-collar ghetto of traditionally low-paying, or nonpaying, dead-end jobs. Charlotte Taylor owns a management consulting firm, CTA Management Group, in Washington, DC. She is also the Former Executive Director of the Presidential Task Force on Women Business Owners. Order from Center on Education and Training for Employment, 1900 Kenny Rd., Columbus, OH 43210.

B6.   *Executive Derailment: A Study of Top Corporate Women.* Greensboro, NC: Center on Creative Leadership, 1985.

> Summarizes the Executive Women Project, which was concerned with finding better ways for companies to select and develop women as well as men for key executive posts. Order from P.O. Box P–1, Greensboro, NC 27402.

B7.   *Executive Mentoring.* N. Mertz, O. Welch, and J. Henderson. Newton, MA: WEEA Publishing Center, 1990.

Identifies the nature of mentoring from the perspective of the mentor. Assesses mentors' needs, defines the problems they face, and examines the role mentoring plays in their organizations. Includes such topics as why mentor, what is in it for you, how to select a protégé, how to begin and end a mentoring relationship, how to structure the relationship, and what to consider when mentoring women and people of color. Order from 55 Chapel St., Suite 200, Newton, MA 02160.

B8. *Female Management Style.* Annotated bibliography. New York: Catalyst, 1985.

Lists 20 articles, research reports, and books that provide a survey of recent research on women managers. Order from 250 Park Ave. South, New York, NY 10003.

B9. *Female Management Style: Myth and Reality.* New York: Catalyst, 1986.

Reports that gender differences in managerial style may be mainly in the eye of the beholder. Order from 250 Park Ave. South, NY 10003.

B10. *Feminine Leadership or How to Succeed in Business Without Being One of the Boys.* Marilyn Loden. New York: Times Books, 1985.

Counsels women on how to develop their natural skills for an effective feminine leadership style. Defines the unique style of women managers and challenges the philosophy of female emulation of the traditional masculine leadership model.

B11. *The Glass Ceiling: A Closer Look.* New York: Catalyst, 1987.

Discusses previously unexplored dimensions of the barriers to women's career growth. Order from 250 Park Ave. South, New York, NY 10003.

B12. *I Can Do It! The American Entrepreneur Series.* Videocassette. Los Angeles, CA: Direct Cinema, 1985.

Contains three "I Can Do It" film units that may be used separately or in sequence. Each unit is planned to take one

hour to complete. The three units are "Owning Your Own
Business" (Ed Lewis—Printing Company), "Starting Your
Own Business" (Judi Wineland—adventure travel business),
and "Building Your Own Business" (Stew Leonard—Dairy
Store). A unit entitled "Planning Your Own Business" has
students apply what they have learned to develop a plan for
a new business. Includes teacher's guide. Order from P.O.
Box 69589, Los Angeles, CA 90069.

B13.   "Men and Women as Managers: A Significant Case of
No Significant Difference." Susan M. Donnell and Jay Hall.
Organizational Dynamics, Spring 1980, 60–77.

Presents the findings of the author's study of nearly 2,000
managers to uncover any true differences between the management style and effectiveness of men and women managers.

B14.   *More Statistical Surprises*. Pamphlet. New York: Catalyst, 1987.

Presents common perceptions and statistical realities on nontraditional careers, choosing career and/or family, managerial
styles, entrepreneurs, directors' qualifications, reaching the
top, and role models. States implications for business planning. Order from 250 Park Ave. South, New York, NY
10003.

B15.   *Reskilling the American Workforce*. Videocassette. Columbus, OH: National Center on Research in Vocational Education, n.d.

Suggests that American business and industry should make
a long-term commitment to reskilling their employees to
keep pace with rapidly changing technology and increased
foreign competition, and that public policy should encourage this practice by providing incentives to invest in human
capital. Because of the post–World War II baby boom, today's work force will be tomorrow's work force for some
time. Maintaining America's competitive edge will depend
on how well these workers can adapt to tomorrow's workplace. Commentary by Dr. Pat Choate of TRW. Order from

Center on Education and Training for Employment, 1900 Kenny Rd., Columbus, OH 43210.

B16. *Risk to Riches: Women and Entrepreneurship in America, a Special Report.* Edie Fraser. Washington, DC: Institute for Enterprise Advancement, 1986.

Profiles prominent women entrepreneurs in the country's top 18 industries.

B17. "Sky's the Limit for Women." Judi Mottaz. *Alton Telegraph*, 31 Jan. 1985, sec. A–12.

Recommends business ownership for women as a way to make more money, secure tax benefits, and break out of the "women's jobs" mold.

B18. "Training and Developing Women Managers: Are They Really a Special Case?" Michael D. Ames and Dorothy Heide. *Personnel Administrator*, Nov. 1982, 19–26.

Addresses the following questions: Are women managers really different? Do aspiring women managers need to be trained differently than aspiring men managers? And do managers need to be trained to deal with physical, psychological, or gender role differences between themselves and their peers?

B19. "Vive La Différence? In Business World, Quelle Différence?" Jennifer Bingham Hull. *Wall Street Journal*, 5 Sept. 1984.

Questions whether there are real differences for men and women employed in business.

B20. *Vocational Education and Business: A Partnership That Works.* Brochure. Washington, DC: National Alliance of Business, n.d.

Describes for businesses how a partnership with the vocational education system in their community may be beneficial. Order from Center on Vocational Education—Business Cooperation, 1015 15th St., NW, Suite 500, Washington, DC 20005.

B21. "Wage Equity in Business and Office Occupations." Helen Carl. *Journal of Education for Business*, Jan. 1986, 168–69.

Outlines a brief history of the unionization of business and office occupations and the contributions of feminist organizations, trade associations, legislative bodies, and wage equity groups toward the achievement of equitable pay for women in office occupations.

B22.   *The Woman Entrepreneur.* Robert D. Hisrich and Candida G. Brush. Lexington, MA: Lexington Books, 1986.

Provides a guide for women considering starting, financing, and managing a successful new business. Order from D.C. Heath and Company, Lexington Books, Lexington, MA 02173.

B23.   *Woman's Place Is at the Typewriter.* Margery W. Davies. Santa Rosa, CA: National Women's History Project, 1982.

Chronicles office work and office workers from 1870 to 1930. Order from P.O. Box 3716, Santa Rosa, CA 95402.

B24.   *Women and Office Automation: Issues for the Decade Ahead.* Women's Bureau. Pamphlet. Washington, DC: U.S. Department of Labor, n.d.

Discusses how new office technologies impact clerical work and affect the day-to-day work life of clerical workers. Order from U.S. Department of Labor, Office of the Secretary, Women's Bureau, 200 Constitution Ave., NW, Washington, DC 20210.

B25.   *Women and Relocation: Probing Assumptions.* Pamphlet. New York: Catalyst, 1987.

Discusses Catalyst's investigation into decision makers' perceptions of women as candidates for relocation and the extent to which women are willing to relocate. Order from 250 Park Ave. South, New York, NY 10003.

B26.   *Women and the Business Game: Strategies for Successful Ownership.* Charlotte Taylor. Washington, DC: Venture Concepts, 1980.

Explains business skills necessary for women to overcome obstacles facing women in business and to start and successfully operate their own business.

B27.   "Women and the Executive Suite." Lynn Langway et al. *Newsweek,* 14 Sept. 1981, 65–68.

Considers how growing numbers of women are overcoming barriers to succeed as business managers.

B28. *Women Business Owners: Selling to the Federal Government.* Becky Norton Dunlop. Washington, DC: U.S. Small Business Administration, 1984.

Guides women business owners by providing information about the marketing of goods and services to the federal government. Includes an agency resources bibliography. Order from U.S. Small Business Administration, Office of Women's Business Ownership, Washington, DC 20416.

B29. *Women Entrepreneurs: A Corporate Brain Drain?* Pamphlet. New York: Catalyst, 1986.

Addresses the issue of women dropping out of corporations to start their own businesses. Order from 250 Park Ave. South, New York, NY 10003.

B30. "Women in Business." *Best of Business* 7.2 (Fall 1985): 53–71.

Includes the special reports "Women's Long March to the Top," by Liz Roman Gallese; "Coping with Comparable Worth," by George P. Sape; and "The 'Forgotten Husband' Syndrome," by Bebe Moore Campbell.

B31. *Women in Business.* Videocassette. Los Angeles, CA: Direct Cinema, 1980.

Introduces audiences to different types of women business owners, each with her own perspective on her work. A film for anyone who is interested in entrepreneurship or the changing role of women in American business. An excellent way to start discussion about the problems and the promises of running a business. Speaks to women of all ages and backgrounds, letting them know that business success can be a reality in their own lives. Order from P.O. Box 69589, Los Angeles, CA 90069.

B32. *Women Working Home.* Marion Behr and Wendy Lazar. Edison, NJ: Women Working Home, 1983.

Provides a business guide and directory geared to the home-based entrepreneur. Discusses choosing a home business, simplified record keeping, the IRS and home business, computer systems for home business use, setting fair prices for products and services, successful marketing, pricing formula for crafts, and turning volunteer skills into marketable skills. Lists a nationwide network of home-based businesswomen. Order from 24 Fishel Rd., Edison, NJ 08820.

3

Career Guidance (CG)

CG1. *Achieving Sex Equity Through Social Studies Grades K–6.* Curriculum guide. Washington, DC: Public Schools of the District of Columbia, 1984.

> Explores sex roles, career aspirations, and sex fairness in grades K–3 and growing up female and male, exclusion, and sex fairness in vocational education for grades 4–6. Competency based. Order from Office of Sex Equity in Vocational Education, 415 12th St., NW, Room 1010, Washington, DC 20004.

CG2. *Achieving Sex Equity Through Social Studies Grades 7–12.* Curriculum guide. Washington, DC: Public Schools of the District of Columbia, 1984.

> Explores awareness in grades 7–9 and civil rights regulations and women in history for grades 10–12. Competency based. Order from Office of Sex Equity in Vocational Education, 415 12th St., NW, Room 1010, Washington, DC 20004.

CG3. *Alternatives to Sex-Restrictive Vocational Interest Assessment.* D. J. Prediger and R. W. Johnson. Iowa City, IA: ACT Publications, 1979.

> Summarizes research on sex restrictiveness in interest assessment procedures. Order from P.O. Box 168, Iowa City, IA 52243.

CG4. *Black Women in a High-Tech World.* Washington, DC: Project in Equal Education Rights, 1982.

> Reports on concerns of African-American women preparing for jobs in a high-tech world. Order from 99 Hudson St., 12th Floor, New York, NY 10013.

CG5. *Career Decision-Making System.* Thomas F. Harrington and Arthur J. O'Shea. Circle Pines, MN: American Guidance Service, 1984.

> Contains a career decision-making exercise. Order from American Guidance Service, Publishers' Building, Circle Pines, MN 55014.

CG6. *Career Decisions.* Filmstrip. New York: J. C. Penney Consumer Education Services, 1983.

Portrays the many influences on job choice. Concludes that vocational maturation is based on understanding oneself, processing adequate up-to-date job information, and an awareness of the opportunities possible in the world of work. Order from 1301 Avenue of the Americas, New York, NY 10019.

CG7. *Career Development.* Filmstrip/audiotape. New York: J. C. Penney Consumer Education Services, 1983.

Heighten's awareness of work and stimulates exploration of work values. Objectives are to provide information for educators about career education; to provide an opportunity to discuss work values, attitudes, and beliefs about work and leisure; to provide learning experiences that will help the participants identify their concepts of work; and to provide value clarification activities. Order from 1301 Avenue of the Americas, New York, NY 10019.

CG8. "Career Education." Women's Action Alliance. *Equal Play Magazine* 5.1 (Fall 1984).

Devotes entire issue to the successes and failures of the educational system in the effort to implement sex-fair career education. Order from 370 Lexington Ave., New York, NY 10017.

CG9. *Career Education Resource Kit.* Schadell Woolridge. Newton, MA: WEEA Publishing Center, 1984.

Provides products to help counselors in rural areas develop an effective nonsexist career counseling program within limited budgets. Includes an annotated bibliography of nonsexist resources. Order from 55 Chapel St., Suite 200, Newton, MA 02160.

CG10. *Career Planning Curriculum Guide for Adults.* Li Anne Grefsheim. Madison, WI: University of Wisconsin, 1992.

Provides a 72-hour course that uses the National Career Development Guidelines for Adults as the framework of competencies and indicators. Emphasis is on new and reentry workers, single parents, displaced homemakers, JTPA clients, AFDC recipients, and dislocated workers. Contains three modules, one each on self-knowledge, career exploration, and career planning. Includes instructor's notes, handouts, and activity sheets. Order from Center on Education and Work, University of Wisconsin-Madison, Department AM, 1025 W. Johnson St., Madison, WI 53706.

CG11. *Career Planning for Minority Women.* Stanlie M. Jackson. Newton, MA: WEEA Publishing Center, 1982.

Gives women direction and purpose when they look for jobs. Six workshop sessions based on the actual experience of minority women direct participants to investigate various careers, analyze their skills, discuss common goals and problems, and ask basic questions. Order from 55 Chapel St., Suite 200, Newton, MA 02160.

CG12. *Career Planning Programs for Women Employees: Review of the Literature.* Patricia Worthy-Winkfield, Cheryl Meredith Lowry, and Louise Vetter. R and D Series no. 134. Columbus, OH: National Center for Research in Vocational Education, 1977.

Reviews the status of women in the labor force, the relationship between socialization and careers, career development theories, and women's career patterns. Order from Center on Education and Training for Employment, 1900 Kenny Rd., Columbus, OH 43215.

CG13. *Catalyst Career Opportunities Series for Women.* New York: Catalyst, n.d.

Includes a series of 40 briefs and two career-planning booklets designed to offer current and comprehensive information about different occupations. Each career brief is about 10 pages long and contains a profile of an individual in a specific job and facts about the industry in general, including salary levels and education and training needed. Order from 250 Park Ave. South, New York, NY 10003.

CG14. *The Catalyst Training Package: Increasing Options for Rural Youth.* Ned Straus and Lynn Walther. Newton, MA: WEEA Publishing Center, 1982.

Contains training programs for rural educators, students, and community residents. Has a successful track record as a tool to help students and community groups examine career choices and eliminate gender role stereotypes. Order from 55 Chapel St., Suite 200, Newton, MA 02160.

CG15. *Choices.* Janis VanBuren. Videocassette. West Lafayette, IN: Purdue University, 1989.

Focuses on our rapidly changing society and on the need for individuals to make wise choices in their high school years. Addresses the issues of gender equity, emphasizing that all individuals should have equal access to training and employment that results in equal pay. Pictures high school students around the lunch table discussing these equity topics. Order from Illinois State Curriculum Center, Sangamon State University, Springfield, IL 62794.

CG16. *Choices: A Teen Woman's Journal for Self Awareness and Personal Planning.* Mindy Bingham, Judy Edmondson, and Sandy Stryker. El Toro, CA: Mission Publications, 1985.

Addresses the problems teenage men and women encounter as they move toward adulthood. Designed to help students think about the future, set goals, clarify values, make sound decisions, assert themselves, and evaluate career choices. Companion to *Challenges: A Young Man's Journal for Self Awareness and Personal Planning* (M). Instructor's guide and student workbook available. Order from P.O. Box 25, El Toro, CA 92630.

CG17. "Choices and Challenges." Mindy Bingham. *Workplace Education,* May/June 1986, 6–7.

Explains why young women need to prepare for their own future economic security and promotes the *Choices* and *Challenges* curricula.

CG18. *Choosing Occupations and Life Roles.* Karen J. Pffiffner. 4 vols. Newton, MA: WEEA Publishing Center, 1983.

Combats stereotyped thinking about jobs and job selection. Order from 55 Chapel St., Suite 200, Newton, MA 02160.

CG19. *Collected Papers: Educational Equity Issues in Community Colleges.* Carol J. Gross. Newton, MA: WEEA Publishing Center, 1978.

> Enlightens community college women as it examines women's career preparation, especially in vocational training and nontraditional jobs. Order from 55 Chapel St., Suite 200, Newton, MA 02160.

CG20. *Commitment and the Young Recruit.* New York: Catalyst, 1985.

> Considers whether today's recruits are less committed. Focuses on guidance counseling for females. Order from 250 Park Ave. South, New York, NY 10003.

CG21. *Connections: Women and Work and Skills for Good Jobs.* Vivian Guilfoy. Newton, MA: WEEA Publishing Center, 1981.

> Contains fresh, fun, and practical lessons about work and careers. Includes a game book with lessons, exercises, and hands-on experiences designed to shake boys and girls out of stereotyped, narrow notions of careers; a leader's guide that provides background information, insightful discussion questions, and suggestions for implementation; and *Women at Work*, a sound filmstrip with script in which three women in nontraditional careers describe their work and explain how they prepared for their careers. Order from 55 Chapel St., Suite 200, Newton, MA 02160.

CG22. *Equity/Nontraditional Career Recruitment and Counseling: A Bibliography.* Rebecca Augustyniak. Tallahassee, FL: Florida State University, 1987.

> Contains information on career counseling, employment qualifications, educational needs, career guidance, career choice, and job placement. Order from Florida Educational Information Service, Center on Instructional Development and Services, Tallahassee, FL 32306.

CG23. *Expanded Career Choices: Curriculum Guide.* Pat Gosz. St. Paul, MN: State Board of Vocational Technical Education, 1985.

> Provides 15 units of instruction to assist in the development of lifelong career plans. Designed to meet the needs of indi-

viduals entering or reentering the job market. Order from State Board of Vocational Technical Education, St. Paul, MN 55101.

CG24. *Expanding Career Options Counselor Workshop.* Joyce Fouts, Jim Mahrt, and Suzanne Lewandowski. Wayne, MI: Network Project, 1986.

Contains a one-day training guide designed to increase counselor awareness of sex bias and gender role stereotyping on career choice and male-female relationships. Activities are especially designed for counselors. Several checklists, guide sheets, and role-playing situations help counselors recognize sex bias and deal with it in an affirmative way. Pilot-tested in Michigan schools. Balanced male/female focus. Order from Wayne County Intermediate School District, 33500 Van Born Rd., Wayne, MI 48184.

CG25. *Exploring Military Service for Women.* Mary McGowan Slappey. New York: Rosen Publishing Group, 1986.

Describes career options for women in various branches of the armed services. Includes eligibility and enlistment requirements, rules and regulations, personal achievements, and future career possibilities.

CG26. *Facts and Reflections on Careers for Today's Girls.* Indianapolis, IN: Girls Clubs of America, 1985.

Reviews literature that integrates the information bearing on girls' preparation for the workplace. Order from National Resource Center, 441 W. Michigan St., Indianapolis, IN 46202.

CG27. *Fair Play: Developing Self-Concept and Decision-Making Skills in the Middle School (Decisions about Roles).* Byron G. Massialas. Newton, MA: WEEA Publishing Center, 1983.

Explores occupational aspirations, expectations, and decision-making skills in a program of social studies. Implementation handbook available. Order from 55 Chapel St., Suite 200, Newton, MA 02160.

CG28. *Film/Videotape Bibliography for the Technical Assistance Center of the Southwest.* Nacogdoches, TX: Stephen F. Austin State University, 1985.

Provides a listing of films and videotapes related to sex and race desegregation, human relations, and career education. Order from Technical Assistance Center of the Southwest, Stephen F. Austin State University, Nacogdoches, TX 75961.

CG29. *A Guide to Counseling Programs Which Enhance Gender Free Career and Course Selection.* Alvin Evans. Cleveland, OH: Cleveland Public Schools, 1984.

Provides representative materials to assist in eliminating sex bias and gender role stereotyping in student enrollment in courses, classes, or activities. Order from Department of Curriculum and Instruction, Cleveland, OH 44101.

CG30. *High-Tech Career Strategies for Women.* Joan Rachel Goldberg. New York: Macmillan, 1984.

Provides a guide to finding a job and getting ahead in today's fastest growing industries. Order from 866 Third Ave., New York, NY 10022.

CG31. *It's Your Future! Catalyst's Career Guide for High School Girls.* New York: Catalyst, 1984.

Includes self-discovery exercises, anecdotes about the experiences of working women, and friendly advice to encourage girls to identify their needs, interests, skills, and values, and to plan for their future work and family lives. Order from 250 Park Ave. South, New York, NY 10003.

CG32. *Jobs for the Future.* Washington, DC: U.S. Department of Labor, 1987.

Discusses the changes occurring in the workplace and provides women with resources for making career choices. Order from U.S. Department of Labor, Office of the Secretary, Women's Bureau, 200 Constitution Ave., NW, Washington, DC 20210.

CG33. *Life Planning Education.* Carol Hunter-Geboy, Lynn Peterson, Sean Casey, Leslie Hardy, and Sarah Renner. Washington, DC: Center on Population Options, 1985.

Focuses on two of the most important tasks teens face: preparing for the world of work and dealing with their sexual and reproductive development, feelings, and behaviors. Order from 1012 14th St., NW, Suite 1200, Washington, DC 20005.

CG34. *Look Sharp.* Videocassette. Roseburg, OR: Umpqua Training and Employment, n.d.

Demonstrates the importance and impact of appearance when looking for a job. Covers such topics as employers' standards for job applicants, how to afford what it takes to make a good appearance on a limited budget, and tips on wardrobe, hair, and makeup. VHS, 30 min. Order from 880 S.E. Jackson, Roseburg, OR 97470.

CG35. *Minority Women's Survival Kit: Personal and Professional Development for Minority Women.* Stanlie M. Jackson. Newton, MA: WEEA Publishing Center, 1982.

Examines critical issues from the perspective of minority women—their needs, their anxieties, and their hopes. Four workshops, each two and one-half hours in length, cover the most pressing issues of survival: discrimination, human rights, employment rights, communication skills, labor laws, interviewing techniques, and job-hunting skills. Order from 55 Chapel St., Suite 200, Newton, MA 02160.

CG36. *Mirror/Mirror.* Videocassette. Charleston, WV: West Virginia Department of Education, 1990.

Pictures a girl talking to her reflection in a mirror about what career she would like to pursue. Emphasizes taking all the math and science courses possible and following a nontraditional career. Order from Bureau of Adult Technical Education, Charleston, West VA 25414.

CG37. *New Directions for Rural Women: A Workshop Leader's Manual.* Mary Gindhart. Newton, MA: WEEA Publishing Center, 1979.

Provides a counseling program for rural women that recognizes their diversity and their particular needs. Provides formats for workshops on career development, personal growth, assertiveness, political participation, legal rights, and the preservation of rural values. Order from 55 Chapel St., Suite 200, Newton, MA 02160.

CG38. *Options: A Career Development Curriculum for Rural High School Students.* Faith Dunne. Newton, MA: WEEA Publishing Center, 1980.

Introduces rural students to careers and explains the basics of job hunting. The basic curriculum applies to rural areas in the Midwest. Each unit includes a teacher's guide and transparency masters. Unit 1, "Understanding People in Our Area," enables students to explore the kinds of decisions they will have to make if they remain in their home locale. Unit 2, "Decision Making," offers students the opportunity to learn to cope with problems defined in the first unit. Unit 3, "Life Planning," uses a simulation game to encourage students to consider the consequences of various decisions they make. Unit 4, "The Juggling Act—Lives and Careers," uses case studies to teach students to handle complex family and work situations. Order from 55 Chapel St., Suite 200, Newton, MA 02160.

CG39. "A Practical Approach to Career and Life Planning for Teen Women: A Case History of the Development of the 'Choices' Curriculum." Barbara B. Greene and Mindy Bingham. *Youth and Society* 16.3 (Mar. 1985): 357–74.

Defines the steps and rationale for the widely used *Choices* curriculum.

CG40. *Preparing for the Jobs of the 1990's: What You Should Know.* Videocassette. Beacon, NY: Guidance Associates, 1986.

Outlines how to develop a flexible approach to career preparation. Focuses on key factors that can change the job market, including the current computer revolution, and describes numerous valuable resources for career planning. Includes a program guide. Order from 579 South Ave., Beacon, NY 12508.

CG41. *Rainbow Shave Ice, Crackseed, and Other Ono Stuff.* Honolulu, HI: University of Hawaii, 1984.

Contains an activity guide of short activities that will raise the awareness of students about bias-free exploration and selection of jobs and careers. Order from Office of the State

Director for Vocational Education, 2327 Dole St., Honolulu, HI 96822.

CG42. *Rainbow Shave Ice . . . Second Serving.* Honolulu, HI: University of Hawaii, 1985.

Promotes the exploration of careers without the limitation of gender role stereotypes and biases through use of a compilation of information and classroom activities. Supplement to *Rainbow Shave Ice, Crackseed, and Other Ono Stuff* (CG). Order from Office of the State Director for Vocational Education, 2327 Dole St., Honolulu, HI 96822.

CG43. *So You Want to Go to Work.* Fairfield, CT: General Electric Company, 1985.

Describes eleven broad categories of work possibilities. Aimed at high school students. Photographs are sex-fair. Order from General Electric Company, Educational Communications Program, Fairfield, CT 06431.

CG44. *Steppin' Up and Moving On: A Career Education Program for the Urban, Noncollege-Bound Student.* Patricia A. Fisher. Newton, MA: WEEA Publishing Center, 1982.

Describes a vigorous transitional program for noncollege-bound students that addresses urban minority students and emphasizes women. Order from 55 Chapel St., Suite 200, Newton, MA 02160.

CG45. "Through the Career-Book Maze." Shirley Sloan Fader. *Working Woman,* Nov. 1984, 83–84.

Contains reviews of several good career books.

CG46. "Toward Sex-Fair Assessment of Vocational Interests." Dale J. Prediger. *VocEd,* Apr. 1980.

Gives suggestions on what to do about the problem of sex bias in vocational interest assessment.

CG47. *What to Do with the Rest of Your Life: The Catalyst Career Guide for Women in the '80s.* New York: Catalyst, 1980.

Offers career planning advice and comprehensive information on a variety of career fields. A career guide for women who want to plan, begin, change, or advance in a promising career. Includes exercises to help the reader clarify skills,

interests, and values, set goals, and make career decisions. Order from 250 Park Ave. South, New York, NY 10003.
CG48. *When Can You Start? The Complete Job Search Guide for Women of All Ages.* New York: Catalyst, 1981.
> Includes topics on setting goals, researching careers, writing letters and resumes, interviewing, and evaluating job offers. Provides step-by-step job search strategies for women at every stage of their careers. Order from 250 Park Ave. South, New York, NY 10003.

CG49. *The Whole Person Book (I): Toward Self-Discovery and Life Options.* Twila Christensen Liggett, Patricia L. Stevens Romero, and Nan Schweiger Schmeling. Newton, MA: WEEA Publishing Center, 1979.
> Guides students through activities designed to examine their personal values, talents, and interests. Students practice matching their skills and personalities with job requirements and, through discussions and questions, probe the personal and social reasons for their career choices. Complements programs in social studies, home economics, psychology, and vocational education. Order from 55 Chapel St., Suite 200, Newton, MA 02160.

CG50. *The Woman Within.* Lorraine Rea. Newton, MA: WEEA Publishing Center, 1981.
> Includes eight workshop sessions to build self-image and self-esteem by suggesting and nurturing behavioral change. Contains inventive role-playing activities, worksheets, and discussions that keep each session lively and stimulating. Order from 55 Chapel St., Suite 200, Newton, MA 02160.

CG51. *Women and Work: Paths to Power.* Nancy M. Laitman-Ashley. Columbus, OH: National Center on Research in Vocational Education, 1979.
> Presents proceedings of a symposium that explored major problems women encounter in career and job transitions and offered strategies and opportunities to solve them. Order from Center on Education and Training for Employment, 1900 Kenny Rd., Columbus, OH 43215.

CG52. *Women in Management.* Irene Place. Lincolnwood, IL: VGM Career Horizons, 1980.
> Provides a career development manual discussing women in management and leadership positions.

CG53. *Women on the Job: Careers in the Electronic Media.* Washington, DC: American Women in Radio and Television, 1984.
> Provides awareness information for women about the new jobs available in the changing field of media. Order from 1321 Connecticut Ave., NW, Washington, DC 20036.

CG54. *A Word in Edgewise.* Heather Macleod. Videocassette. New York: Women Make Movies, 1986.
> Focuses on language bias and on ways vocabulary is being affected by women's changing roles in society. Points out how we need to transform the way we perceive and use language. Discusses the history of language bias, language implications, the use of *he* and *she*, and the labeling of women according to their relationships to men. Order from Illinois State Curriculum Center, Sangamon State University, Springfield, IL 62794.

CG55. "Youth and Society." Heather Johnston Nicholson. *Youth and Society* 16.3 (Mar. 1985).
> Devotes entire issue to careers for today's girls and young women.

4

Communications (CM)

CM1. "Are All Men Equal? The 'Generic' Dilemma." Carolyn Bocella Bagin. *Simply Stated*, Jan. 1986, 1–2.

> Considers the use of the generic *he*. Order from Document Design Center, American Institutes for Research, 1055 Thomas Jefferson St., NW, Washington, DC 20007.

CM2. *Closing the Communications Gender Gap.* Rosemary Agonito. Pamphlet. Syracuse, NY: New Futures Enterprises, 1985.

> Uses a question-and-answer format to define the communications gender gap and to suggest solutions to help narrow it. Order from 4502 Broad Rd., Syracuse, NY 13215.

CM3. *Count Me In!* Joyce S. Kaser. Pamphlet. Washington, DC: Network, 1985.

> Provides guidelines for enhancing participation in mixed gender work groups. Order from Mid-Atlantic Center for Sex Equity, 5010 Wisconsin Ave., NW, Suite 310, Washington, DC 20016.

CM4. *Father Gander Nursery Rhymes: The Equal Rhymes Amendment.* Santa Barbara, CA: Advocacy, 1985.

> Applies the delights of the old Mother Goose rhymes to the ideals we want our children to have—equality, love, responsibility, an appreciation of life and all living things, good nutrition, and conservation of resources. Order from P.O. Box 236, Santa Barbara, CA 93102.

CM5. "How Books Influence Children: What the Research Shows." Patricia B. Campbell and Jeana Wirtenberg. *Bulletin* 11.6 (1980): 3–6.

> Shows that children's attitudes and achievements are affected by race and sex bias in books and that unbiased books make a difference.

CM6. *Identifying Sexism and Racism in Children's Books.* 2 filmstrips. New York: Council on Interracial Books for Children, n.d.

Demonstrates for teachers, librarians, day care staff, parents, and college students the blatant and subtle ways in which racist and sexist messages are transmitted to children through the books they read. Offers criteria for selection of books for children. Order from 1841 Broadway, New York, NY 10023.

CM7. *Language and Textbooks.* Anne Grant. Videocassette. Newton, MA: WEEA Publishing Center, 1979.

Examines the impressions children receive from sexist language in their textbooks. Funded by a Women's Educational Equity Act grant and part of the *Venture Beyond Stereotypes* program (GS). Order from 55 Chapel St., Suite 200, Newton, MA 02160.

CM8. *Maximizing Young Children's Potential: A Non-Sexist Manual for Early Childhood Trainers.* Barbara Sprung. Newton, MA: WEEA Publishing Center, 1980.

Details activities and strategies that foster independence and expand children's experiences. Offers useful suggestions for getting parents involved. Order from 55 Chapel St., Suite 200 Newton, MA 02160.

CM9. "Networks: A Matrix for Exchange." *J. C. Penney Forum*, 1983.

Covers such topics as "Discovering Networking," "Redefining Self as a Resource," "Networks that Work," and "Synergy." For vocational educators. Order from J. C. Penney, 1301 Avenue of the Americas, New York, NY 10019.

CM10. "Sex Equity in Bilingual Education, English as a Second Language, and Foreign Language Instruction." Mary L. Spencer and Paula Gilbert Lewis. *Theory Into Practice* 25.4 (Autumn 1986): 257–66.

Outlines differences in language instruction for males and females.

CM11. "Sexism's Universal Curriculum." Kathleen Bonk and Joann Evans Gardner. *American Education*, July 1977, 15–19.

Discusses television's influence in perpetuating sexist notions.

CM12. *Ten Quick Ways to Analyze Children's Books for Racism and Sexism.* Pamphlet. New York: Council on Interracial Books for Children, n.d.

> Describes 10 items to consider when evaluating children's books for racism and sexism. Order from 1841 Broadway, New York, NY 10023.

CM13. "Two Women, Three Men on a Raft." Robert Schrank. *Harvard Business Review,* 55.3 (May/June 1977): 100–108.

> Relates a participant's story of what an Outward Bound raft trip taught him about the relationships between men and women at work.

CM14. *Unlocking Your Potential.* Videocassette. Tacoma, WA: Edge Learning Institute, n.d.

> Includes 10 20-minute units on four video modules. Helps secondary students improve self-esteem, set realistic goals, motivate themselves, and improve communication and decision-making skills, among other goals. Includes students' and facilitator's guides. Order from 7171 W. 27th St., Tacoma, WA 98466.

CM15. *Was It Something I Said?* Brochure. Springfield, IL: Illinois State Board of Education, 1985.

> Promotes the use of unbiased language with biased and sex-fair examples. Order from the Department of Adult, Vocational, and Technical Education, 100 N. First St., Springfield, IL 62777.

5

Computers (CP)

CP1. "Beyond Equal Access: Gender Equity in Learning with Computers." June Mark. *WEEA Digest*, June 1992, 1–2, 6–7.

> Contends that gender differences have been documented in computer use and access; girls are more likely to use computers for word processing, boys for programming. Considers informal settings, math and science, learning experiences, and software. Provides strategies for designing instruction and access that is equitable. Order from 55 Chapel St., Suite 200, Newton, MA 02160.

CP2. *Cave Girl Clair.* Computer software. Rhiannon Software/ Adventure Stories for Girls. Reading, MA: Addison-Wesley, 1984.

> Helps girls become familiar with computer keyboards and develop computer literacy. Unlike alien-zapping computer games, Rhiannon Software encourages creativity and problem solving along with computer skills. Alone in prehistoric times, Cave Girl Clair must learn to gather food and tend fire to survive. Order from 3717 Titan Dr., Richmond, VA 23225.

CP3. *Chelsea of the South Sea Islands.* Computer software. Rhiannon Software/Adventure Stories for Girls. Reading, MA: Addison-Wesley, 1984.

> Provides an exciting nonviolent avenue to help girls become familiar with computer keyboards and develop computer literacy. Encourages creativity and problem solving. A nineteenth-century British girl is stranded on a tropical island and surrounded by danger. She must solve problems to survive. Order from 3717 Titan Dr., Richmond, VA 23225.

CP4. *Computer Chips and Paper Clips.* Heidi I. Hartmann, Robert E. Kraut, and Louise A. Tilly, eds. Washington, DC: National Academy Press, 1986.

> Provides information on the relationship between technology and women's employment, including findings and rec-

ommendations for further research. Order from 2101 Constitution Ave., NW, Washington, DC 20418.

CP5. "Computer Equity." Women's Action Alliance. *Equal Play Magazine* 4.1–2 (Spring/Fall 1983).

> Considers the importance of computer equity in our educational system. Order from 370 Lexington Ave., New York, NY 10017.

CP6. *The DPMA Secondary Curriculum on Information Technology and Computer Information Systems.* Park Ridge, IL: Data Processing Management Association, 1984.

> Describes curriculum designed to respond to the needs of secondary students for computer literacy, marketable, computer-related skills in occupational education programs, and increased knowledge about computer information systems, to meet more stringent college entrance requirements. Order from 505 Busse Highway, Park Ridge, IL 60068.

CP7. "Gender Equity in Computer Learning." Jane G. Schubert. *Theory into Practice* 25.4 (Autumn 1986): 267–75.

> Examines aspects of the school climate that influence students' acquisition of computer experience and the inequity that climate may produce for female students.

CP8. *Integrated Circuits/Segregated Labor: Women in Three Computer-Related Occupations.* Myra H. Strober and Carolyn L. Arnold. Paper. Institute for Research on Educational Finance and Governance. CA: Stanford University, 1984.

> Examines several aspects of gender segregation within three new computer-related occupations.

CP9. *Jenny of the Prairie.* Computer software. Rhiannon Software/Adventure Stories for Girls. Reading, MA: Addison-Wesley, 1984.

> Prepares girls to solve problems creatively while developing computer skills. A brave pioneer girl faces winter alone and must figure out how to survive. Order from 3717 Titan Dr., Richmond, VA 23225.

CP10. *Lauren of the 25th Century.* Computer software. Rhiannon Software/Adventure Stories for Girls. Reading, MA: Addison-Wesley, 1984.

Helps girls become familiar with computer keyboards and encourages creativity and problem solving along with computer skills. Offers various skill levels based on age or ability. Lauren's challenges include maintaining a reclamation project in the desert and protecting fragile life forms. Order from 3717 Titan Dr., Richmond, VA 23225.

CP11. *The Neuter Computer.* Jo Shuchat Sanders and Antonia Stone. Curriculum guide with classroom activities. New York: Neal-Schuman Publishers, 1986.

Includes computer learning activities for all ages and guidelines and strategies for planning and evaluating a computer equity program in school. Funded through Women's Action Alliance. Order from 23 Leonard St., New York, NY 10013.

CP12. *Programming Equity into Computer Education.* Washington, DC: National Center for Computer Equity, 1985.

Presents information as a guide for parents, teachers, administrators, and students who want to find out the extent to which schools support and encourage girls, minority students, students with disabilities, and low-income students to participate in computer education programs and computer-related courses of all kinds. Order from National Center for Computer Equity, NOW Legal Defense and Education Fund, 1413 K St., NW, 9th Floor, Washington, DC 20005.

CP13. *The Report Card 3: Sex Bias in Mathematics, Computer Science, and Technology.* John Lipkin and David Sadker. Washington, DC: Mid-Atlantic Center for Sex Equity, 1983.

Highlights recent research findings related to sex bias and discrimination in mathematics, computer science, and technology. Order from 5010 Wisconsin Ave., NW, Suite 308, Washington, DC 20016.

CP14. *Sex Bias at the Computer Terminal: How Schools Program Girls.* Washington, DC: Project in Equal Education Rights, 1984.

Examines how girls may be missing out on future opportunities in tomorrow's high-tech world because of sex bias in schools. Order from 1413 K St., NW, 9th Floor, Washington, DC 20005.

CP15. *Sex Equity in Computer Education: Concerns for Social Studies.* Lynn Parisi. ERIC Digest no. 15. Boulder CO: ERIC Clearinghouse for Social Studies/Social Science Education, 1984.

> Reviews recent research on gender equity in computer education and addresses the implications of this research for social studies educators. Order from 855 Broadway, Boulder, CO 80302.

CP16. *Technology in the Schools: Equity and Funding.* John C. Arch, ed. Washington, DC: National Education Association, 1986.

> Addresses the issue of equity, particularly computer equity, in technology.

CP17. *What's It Like to Work with Computers?* Fairfield, CT: General Electric Company, 1985.

> Discusses present and future uses of computers in offices, industry, and the home. Describes the major types of computer careers and includes information on how to prepare for computer-related careers. Photographs are sex-fair. Order from General Electric Company, Educational Communications Program, Fairfield, CT 06431.

6 Discrimination (D)

D1. *Comparable Worth: A Workable Approach.* Pamphlet. New York: Catalyst, 1985.

> Considers integrating women into the entire work force as a workable solution to the concept of comparable worth. Order from 250 Park Ave. South, New York, NY 10003.

D2. *Comparable Worth: An Analysis and Recommendations.* Washington, DC: U.S. Commission on Civil Rights, 1985.

> Contains a report of the U.S. Commission on Civil Rights.

D3. *Comparable Worth and the Wage Gap.* Washington, DC: Women's Equity Action League, 1985.

> Analyzes the controversy surrounding the pay equity movement. Adapted from a speech for a seminar at George Washington University. Order from 1250 I St., NW, Suite 305, Washington, DC 20005.

D4. *Comparable Worth: Issue for the 80's.* Washington, DC: U.S. Commission on Civil Rights, 1984.

> Contains a compilation of all papers submitted by consultation participants at the U.S. Commission on Civil Rights consultation in Washington, DC, 6–7 June 1984.

D5. "Comparable Worth: The Working Woman's Issue for the 80's." Beverly Jacobson. *National Forum*, Fall 1981, 5–6.

> Summarizes the highlights of the comparable worth issue.

D6. *Discrimination American Style.* Joe R. Feagin and Clairece Booher Feagin. Englewood Cliffs, NJ: Prentice-Hall, 1978.

> Provides points of view on why and how some people are discriminated against in our society. Order from Route 9-W, Englewood Cliffs, NJ 07632.

D7. *Fact Sheets on Institutional Racism.* New York: Council on Interracial Books for Children, 1984.

> Provides various quotations and statistics on racism, relating to the economy, education, government, health, media, and so on. Order from 1841 Broadway, New York, NY 10023.

D8. *Fact Sheets on Institutional Sexism.* New York: Council on Interracial Books for Children, 1982.
> Provides various quotations and statistics on sexism and racism relating to the economy, education, government, health, media, and so on. Order from 1841 Broadway, New York, NY 10023.

D9. *Fifty-One Questions on the OCR Guidelines.* Raymond E. Harlan. R and D Series no. 205. Columbus, OH: National Center for Research in Vocational Education, 1981.
> Includes a user handbook, a set of transparency masters, and a set of audience handout masters. Designed to aid vocational education personnel in eliminating unlawful discrimination from vocational education programs, services, and activities. Order from Center for Education and Training for Employment, 1900 Kenny Rd., Columbus, OH 43215.

D10. "Forewarned is Forearmed: Potential Between and Within Sex Discrimination." M. A. Hitt and W. G. Zikmund. *Sex Roles* 12.7/8 (Apr. 1985), 807–812.
> Reports on a study of the effect that a woman's display of active interest in equal employment opportunity (a feminist perspective) has on her candidacy for a position. Considers how a personnel manager would likely respond to a person who has shown an interest in equal employment opportunity issues.

D11. *Judge Me, Not My Shell.* Martha Whalen Kent. Videocassette. Newton, MA: WEEA Publishing Center, 1978.
> Dramatizes for middle and secondary students the hardships of belonging to a minority group. For use with *Competence is for Everyone* series (GS). Includes script, discussion questions, and teacher's worksheet. 3/4 in., 15 min. Order from 55 Chapel St., Suite 200, Newton, MA 02160.

D12. *Keeping Track.* Jeannie Oakes. New Haven, CT: Yale University Press, 1985.
> Discusses the idea of "tracking" in schools, the secondary school practice of separating students for instruction by achievement or ability, and its effect on the education of students.

D13. *Pay Equity: An Issue of Race, Ethnicity, and Sex.* Washington, DC: National Committee on Pay Equity, 1987.
Reports on a study that examined occupational segregation in the U.S. work force, focusing on three case studies of wage-setting systems in localities at different stages of pay equity implementation. Order from 1301 16th Street, NW, Suite 422, Washington, DC 20036.

D14. "Reagan's Proposal to Eliminate Affirmative Action Guidelines Draws Fire." *Higher Education Daily*, 20 Sept. 1985, 3–4.
Discusses lobbying efforts against proposed changes in the affirmative action program.

D15. *Responses to Discriminatory Behavior.* Martha McCarthy and Jack Culbertson. Sound filmstrip. Newton, MA: WEEA Publishing Center, n.d.
Examines discriminatory practices faced by women in higher education. Illustrates three resolution techniques: avoidance, confrontation, and legal action. Order from 55 Chapel St., Suite 200, Newton, MA 02160.

D16. "Restrictions Keep Women in Low-Pay Jobs, Study Says." Cathy Trost. *Wall Street Journal*, 12 Dec. 1985.
Discusses the findings in *Women's Work, Men's Work: Sex Segregation on the Job* (D).

D17. "Tests' Sex Bias Costs Women Millions in College Assistance, Group Asserts." Lynn Olson. *Education Week*, Apr. 1987, 5.
Discusses the use of sex-biased examinations in awarding scholarships.

D18. *Update on Women and Girls in America's Schools.* Washington, DC: Project in Equal Education Rights, 1985.
Examines state and national progress in eliminating sex bias in athletic opportunities, vocational education, administrative positions, and computer education. Order from 1413 K St., NW, 9th Floor, Washington, DC 20005.

D19. "Use of Comparable Worth Idea to Fight Job Sex Bias Opposed by Rights Panel." Joann S. Lublin. *Wall Street Journal*, 12 Apr. 1985, 48.

Reports that the U.S. Civil Rights Commission rejected the controversial comparable worth concept as a remedy for sex bias in the workplace.

D20. "Why Can't a Woman's Pay Be More like a Man's?" Bob Arnold. *Business Week,* 28 Jan. 1985, 82–83.

Gives statistics and rationales for differences in pay between men and women. Included in "Women at Work" series (FI).

D21. *Winning Justice for All.* Filmstrip series. New York: Council on Interracial Books for Children, n.d.

Covers social justice issues of sex and race equality in language arts, history, and social studies lesson plan formats. Includes the following filmstrips: *An Equal Chance: Historic and Current Barriers to Sex/Race Equality, Fighting Discrimination: Strategies for Overcoming Sexism and Racism,* and *The Secret of Goodasme: Sex and Race Stereotyping.* For upper elementary students. Includes students' workbook and teacher's edition. Order from 1841 Broadway, New York, NY 10023.

D22. "Women in Management: Fighting Discrimination is Nothing New." *Today's Manager,* Mar. 1986, 6–9.

Presents forms of discrimination that women in management have faced over time.

D23. "Women's Work, Men's Work." Ron Cowen. *NewsReport,* Dec. 1985–Jan. 1986, 4–9.

Summarizes findings of a study by the National Research Council on causes of and possible solutions to sex segregation in the workplace.

D24. *Women's Work, Men's Work: Sex Segregation on the Job.* Barbara F. Reskin and Heidi I. Hartmann. Washington, DC: National Academy Press, 1986.

Reviews evidence that employment segregation by sex has grave consequences for women, men, families, and society, particularly for women. Order from 2101 Constitution Ave., NW, Washington, DC 20418.

D25. "You've Come a Long Way, Baby—But Not as Far as You Thought." *Business Week,* 1 Oct. 1984.

Contends that although discrimination is becoming less overt, women still are not getting to the top.

7

Displaced Homemakers/
Reentry Women (DH)

DH1. *Becoming.* Nancy L. Voight, Alice Cotter Lawler, and Katherine Fee Fulkerson. Newton, MA: WEEA Publishing Center, 1980.

> Kindles ambitions and gives direction to adult women aspiring to become independent and self-sufficient. Designed to complement counseling or teaching. Helps participants understand their motivations, clarify their feelings, and take advantage of educational and employment opportunities. The leader's and participants' guides describe successful techniques for countering racial and sexual bias, coping with stress, and planning for the future. They feature an appendix on antidiscrimination laws and a list of agencies ready to offer assistance. Order from 55 Chapel St., Suite 200, Newton, MA 02160.

DH2. *Better Late Than Never: Financial Aid for Older Women Seeking Education and Training.* Washington, DC: Women's Equity Action League, 1984.

> Identifies scholarships, grants, loans, and other financial aid available to older students. Includes programs for educators and women who want to update credentials, reentry women, and career changers. Order from 1250 I St., NW, Suite 305, Washington, DC 20005.

DH3. *Careers Don't Come in Pink or Blue.* Gail Dunphy. Providence, RI: Division of Women and Human Resources, 1985.

> Teaches students how to explore the many career options available and creates an awareness of how stereotyping and sex bias negatively affect their life choices. A student workbook for displaced homemakers. Order from Rhode Island Department of Community Affairs, Providence, RI 02903.

DH4. *Continuing Education for Women: Administrator's Handbook.* Marjorie M. Parks. Newton, MA: WEEA Publishing Center, 1978.

Provides guidelines for setting up and running an effective counseling service, including budgeting, staffing, and suggestions for developing credit and noncredit programs that meet adult women's needs. Includes appendix with sample forms. Order from 55 Chapel St., Suite 200, Newton, MA 02160.

DH5. *Coordination of Services for Single Parents and Homemakers.* Marian Swisher. Springfield, IL: Illinois State Board of Education, 1986.

Contains the final report on a project to assist single parents and homemakers in acquiring marketable job skills, parenting skills, management skills, and skills in building self-esteem through the coordination of social services and educational services. Order from Department of Adult, Vocational, and Technical Education, 100 N. First St., Springfield, IL 62777.

DH6. *Developing Women's Management Programs: A Guide to Professional Job Reentry for Women.* Judie Zubin. Newton, MA: WEEA Publishing Center, 1982.

Provides a guide for postsecondary administrators who are developing management training programs for reentry women. Helps develop the managerial potential of women and teaches them effective ways of marketing their skills. Describes a self-supporting, 23-week management training program from planning, staffing, and recruiting to developing internships and support networks. Provides an extensive syllabus and a variety of activities. Order from 55 Chapel St., Suite 200, Newton, MA 02160.

DH7. *Discover.* Linda Willson. Sarasota, FL: Women's Resource Center, 1988.

Helps women to confront their fears about change, risk, independence, and decision making and to do so in a supportive, nonjudgmental atmosphere. Includes suggestions and guides for group instruction, individual counseling, career exploration, and vocational and self-concept testing. Order from WEEA Publishing Center, 55 Chapel St., Suite 200, Newton, MA 02160.

DH8. "Displaced Homemakers Find Independence." Victoria Blanchard and Rose Cherry. *VocEd*, Apr. 1985, 33–35.
Describes a comprehensive approach for encouraging displaced homemakers to pursue nontraditional careers.

DH9. *Displaced Homemakers: Vo-Tech Workshop Guide.* Wanda Jo Peltier. Curriculum guide. Newton, MA: WEEA Publishing Center, 1981.
Helps displaced homemakers regain self-confidence. Contains such topics as self-discovery, decision making, and the preparation of resumes, cover letters, and follow-up letters. Order from 55 Chapel St., Suite 200, Newton, MA 02160.

DH10. *Equity Counseling for Community College Women.* Nancy Carol Eliason. Newton, MA: WEEA Publishing Center, 1979.
Shows how to develop outreach and vocational guidance and counseling techniques for minority women and displaced homemakers. Targets many of the two million women who enter community colleges each year, for whom enrollment is an act of courage—they have spent years raising children, many are newly divorced or widowed, and they strive for self-reliance and independence. Developed by counselors at two-year colleges across the nation. Order from 55 Chapel St., Suite 200, Newton, MA 02160.

DH11. *Equity from a Vocational Education Research Perspective.* Nancy Carol Eliason. R and D Series no. 214E. Columbus, OH: National Center for Research in Vocational Education, 1982.
Describes the hidden barriers to full participation by women in vocational education programs, with emphasis on the problems encountered by reentry women. Order from Center on Education and Training for Employment, 1900 Kenny Rd., Columbus, OH 43210.

DH12. *First Step: A Manual for Career Development and Job Seeking Skills.* Curriculum guide. Chicago, IL: Midwest Women's Center, 1986.
Prepares women for placement in a job or training program. Includes prepared lectures, handouts, and group and individ-

ual exercises. Order from 53 W. Jackson Blvd., Suite 1015, Chicago, IL 60604.

DH13. *From Homemaking to Entrepreneurship: A Readiness Training Program.* Washington, DC: U.S. Department of Labor, 1985.

Helps community-based organizations develop and implement for their clients an entrepreneurship training program. Aimed at helping homemakers and other women explore entrepreneurship as a career option and develop the appropriate entrepreneurial attitude. Order from U.S. Department of Labor, Office of the Secretary, Women's Bureau, 200 Constitution Ave., Washington, DC 20210.

DH14. *Greene County Vocational Education Enhancement Project.* Darlene Ridings. Springfield, IL: Illinois State Board of Education, 1986.

Contains the final report on a project to provide special services to increase the number of single parents and homemakers who finish high school, complete their GED, and/ or enroll in vocational education programs. Order from Department of Adult, Vocational, and Technical Education, 100 N. First St., Springfield, IL 62777.

DH15. *Handbook of Employment Skills for Displaced Homemakers.* Springfield, IL: Illinois State Board of Education, 1980.

Assists displaced homemakers with obtaining employment. Order from Curriculum Publications Clearinghouse, Western Illinois University, Horrabin Hall 46, Macomb, IL 61455.

DH16. *How about a Little Strategy?* Gloria Rudolf Frazier. Newton, MA: WEEA Publishing Center, 1980.

Develops problem-solving strategies for women returning to school or entering training programs. Profiles women in crisis and suggests concrete solutions to such problems as finding financial aid, arranging child care, and choosing the most suitable educational program. Also included is an extensive support network of helpful books, pamphlets, and national organizations. Order from 55 Chapel St., Suite 200, Newton, MA 02160.

DH17. *How Women Find Jobs: A Guide for Workshop Leaders.*
Vera Norwood. Newton, MA: WEEA Publishing Center, 1979.
Contains information for women entering or reentering the
work force. Helps the employment counselor set up a practical, effective workshop, and explains how to survey the job
market, publicize the workshop, find students, and lead activities. Students learn to identify their job skills, write resumes,
apply for jobs, go for interviews, and balance work and
home life. Order from 55 Chapel St., Suite 200, Newton,
MA 02160.

DH18. *Learning from Experience: A Handbook for Women.* Audrey Branch. Newton, MA: WEEA Publishing Center, 1982.
Shows the adult working woman how to receive credit for
prior learning, plan for a career, and take advantage of her
maturity and experience. A self-help guide and a companion
to work experience programs. Order from 55 Chapel St.,
Suite 200, Newton, MA 02160.

DH19. *Life Skills for Women in Transition.* Margaret Hunt and
Constance Munro. Newton, MA: WEEA Publishing Center,
1982.
Confronts directly and thoroughly the issues of loneliness,
stress, money, job hunting, battering, communication with
family members, and more. Provides special support and
understanding for women who have limited English skills.
The workshop guide helps counselors, social workers, and
educators set up a class or workshop to build the self-confidence of women during a time of confusion and personal
upheaval. Order from 55 Chapel St., Suite 200, Newton,
MA 02160.

DH20. "Reversing a Trend: Pulling Women from the Poverty
Cycle." Cynthia Davis. *National Business Woman*, Aug./Sept.
1986.
Considers the "feminization of poverty"—the causes and
solutions.

DH21. *Second Wind: A Program for Returning Women Students.* Jane O. Carter. Newton, MA: WEEA Publishing Center,
1978.

Shows how returning women students over the age of 25 can adjust to academic life and remain in school. Features a highly successful plan in which returning students serve as peer counselors and advocates to help their fellow students while strengthening their own leadership skills. Order from 55 Chapel St., Suite 200, Newton, MA 02160.

DH22. *Single Mother's Resource Handbook.* Annette Ferando and David Newbert. Omaha, NE: Head Start Child Development Corp., 1982.

Helps single mothers develop a positive self-image, recognize available alternatives, better express their needs and feelings, positively influence their children, and use problem-solving skills to make better decisions. Order from WEEA Publishing Center, 55 Chapel St., Suite 200, Newton, MA 02160.

DH23. *Single Parents and Homemakers Training Program.* Evelina Jose Cichy. Springfield, IL: Illinois State Board of Education, 1987.

Contains the final report on a program to provide vocational training to single parents and homemakers to enhance their employability. Order from Department of Adult, Vocational, and Technical Education, 100 N. First St., Springfield, IL 62777.

DH24. *Single Parents/Homemakers in Hawaii: A Study of Vocational Education Needs.* Bernard Ostrowski. Honolulu, HI: Department of Education, 1986.

Provides data on vocational education and support needs of single parents and homemakers. Stresses postsecondary vocational education needs. Reports constructed activities, findings, and recommendations. Order from Office of Instructional Services/General Education Branch, Honolulu, HI 96820.

DH25. "Starting Over: Would You Be Happier Doing Something Else?" Lesly Berger. *Working Woman*, June 1985.

Introduces the possibility of changing careers.

DH26. *The Status of Older Women in Illinois Today.* Julia Huiskamp. Springfield, IL: Illinois Department of Aging, 1986.

Examines issues that make it different to grow older as a woman than as a man, with particular attention to housing, health care, and economic security needs.

DH27. *Working with Single-Parent Families.* Florence J. Cherry. Ithaca, NY: Cornell University, [1984?].

Aims to help families recognize their strengths both as individuals and as family members. The goal of this workshop series is to allow participants to voice and examine their concerns as single parents and to gain skills in working through problems and issues they confront on a daily basis. Order from New York State College of Human Ecology, A Statutory College of the State University, Cornell University, Ithaca, NY 14853.

8
Elementary Education (EE)

EE1. *Activities to Raise Student Awareness of Sex Stereotyping.* Harrisburg, PA: Pennsylvania Department of Education, n.d.
> Contains four activities suitable for elementary students. Order from 333 Market St. Harrisburg, PA 17126.

EE2. *Competency Based Curriculum.* Carolyn Dudley, Andrew Hayes, and Edna Mills. Washington, DC: Public Schools of the District of Columbia, 1982.
> Contains competency-based social studies lessons for elementary grades K–6. The overall goal of the project is to ultimately increase enrollment in nontraditional career classes for males and females. Order from Office of Sex Equity in Vocational Education, 415 12th St., NW, Room 1010, Washington, DC 20004.

EE3. "Counteracting Bias in Early Childhood Education." *Bulletin* 14.7–8 (1983).
> Focuses on activities and issues in early childhood education. Order from Council on Interracial Books for Children, 1841 Broadway, New York, NY 10023.

EE4. "Equal Early Education." Women's Action Alliance. *Equal Play Magazine* 1.2–3 (Spring–Summer 1980).
> Reports on the proceedings of the first national meeting of the Institute for Equal Early Education and considers a national effort to create educational equity for all young children. Order from 370 Lexington Ave., New York, NY 10017.

EE5. *Guidelines for Selecting Bias-Free Textbooks and Storybooks.* New York: Council on Interracial Books for Children, 1980.
> Recognizes the importance of children's storybooks and textbooks in shaping attitudes and self-image. The authors prepared this book to help educators and parents select children's books that are free of bias. Order from 1841 Broadway, New York, NY 10023.

EE6. *Holiday Ornaments.* Poster. New York: TABS Aids for Equal Education, n.d.
> Depicts a girl and a boy with their hands in a bowl, mixing dough. The poster text is the recipe for baking dough ornaments. Order from 744 Carroll St., Brooklyn, NY 11215.

EE7. *It's Up to You.* Lynn Stuve. Filmstrip. Newton, MA: WEEA Publishing Center, n.d.
> Teaches preschool and elementary school children about sex bias and gender role stereotyping. Order from 55 Chapel St., Suite 200, Newton, MA 02160.

EE8. *Learning Her Place: Sex Bias in the Elementary School Classroom.* Washington, DC: Project in Equal Education Rights, 1985.
> Considers sex bias in the elementary school classroom. Order from 1413 K St., NW, 9th Floor, Washington, DC 20005.

EE9. *Organizing for Change.* Washington, DC: Project in Equal Education Rights, 1982.
> Contains a step-by-step process, through use of a workbook, that can help community groups carry out a campaign for equal education. Order from 1413 K St., NW, 9th Floor, Washington, DC 20005.

EE10. "Positive and Negative Aspects of Toys." Women's Action Alliance. *Equal Play Magazine* 2.4 (Fall 1981).
> Considers the cultural messages that toy advertising conveys to children and provides teaching ideas, resources, and news of activities that can help children avoid unhealthy messages found packaged in commercial toys. Order from 370 Lexington Ave., New York, NY 10017.

EE11. *Programs for Preadolescents.* Jane Quinn. Washington, DC: Center for Population Options, 1983.
> Describes several successful preadolescent sexuality education programs and outlines guidelines for setting up a new program. Includes resource listing. Order from 2031 Florida Ave., NW, Washington, DC 20009.

EE12. *Sex Equity in Education: NIE-Sponsored Projects and Publications.* Susan S. Klein. Washington, DC: National Institute of Education, 1981.

Provides access to NIE funded research on equal educational opportunities for females and males. Contains 89 abstracts of projects ongoing in 1981 and 272 abstracts of relevant publications sponsored by NIE since 1972.

EE13. *Spatial Encounters.* Peggy Blackwell. Newton, MA: WEEA Publishing Center, 1982.

Enables fun and learning to come together through use of a classroom manual. Boys and girls enjoy visual-spatial games, such as remembering patterns or completing and rotating figures. The exercises contain easy directions for classroom and self-directed use. They show how various visual-spatial skills have applications in the real world of scientific occupations: math, geography, acoustics, landscape architecture, and telecommunications. Order from 55 Chapel St., Suite 200, Newton, MA 02160.

EE14. *Tips and Techniques.* Springfield, IL: Illinois State Board of Education, 1985.

Contains strategies resulting from a symposium held to identify parameters for developing objective, sex-fair standards of measurement for grouping and evaluation in physical education. Order from Title IV Sex Desegregation Project, Equal Educational Opportunity Section, 100 N. First St., Springfield, IL 62777.

EE15. *Women as Members of Committees.* Santa Rosa, CA: National Women's History Project, 1985.

Includes six biographies and illustrations of women, along with appropriate activities, in a specially designed unit in accordance with social studies guidelines. For grade 3. Order from P.O. Box 3716, Santa Rosa, CA 95402.

EE16. *Women as Members of Groups.* Santa Rosa, CA: National Women's History Project, 1985.

Includes six biographies and illustrations of women, along with appropriate activities, in a social studies unit. For grade 2. Order from P.O. Box 3716, Santa Rosa, CA 95402.

EE17. *Women at Work, Home, and School.* Santa Rosa, CA: National Women's History Project, 1985.

Includes six biographies and illustrations of women, along with appropriate activities, in a social studies unit. For grade 1. Order from P.O. Box 3716, Santa Rosa, CA 95402.

EE18. *Working Choices.* Becky Baily and Ann Nihlen. Game. Albuquerque, NM: University of New Mexico, 1985.

Contains a board game for one to four elementary students. Helps them explore nontraditional careers and gives them opportunities to express their feelings about gender role stereotypes. Order from Department of Educational Foundation, University of New Mexico, Albuquerque, NM 87131.

EE19. *You Can Be Anything.* Videocassette. Springfield, IL: Illinois State Board of Education, 1987.

Interviews with men and women working in careers not traditional for their sex. Developed for elementary students. ¾ in., 27 min. Order from Illinois State Curriculum Center, Sangamon State University, Springfield, IL 62794.

9

Family and Work Issues (FW)

FW1. *Addressing Recruits' Work and Family Concerns.* New York: Catalyst, 1987.

> Discusses the need for corporate recruiters to communicate their company's work and family policies to recruits. Order from 250 Park Ave. South, New York, NY 10003.

FW2. *Boosting the Return on Parenting Supports.* New York: Catalyst, 1987.

> Highlights three employers whose communications efforts in parenting support programs are paying dividends. Order from 250 Park Ave. South, New York, NY 10003.

FW3. "Business Starts Tailoring Itself to Suit Working Women." Aaron Bernstein. *Business Week*, 6 Oct. 1986, 50–54.

> Explores how benefits, promotions, and work rules are changing as female employees flood in.

FW4. *Changing Faces of American Families.* Jeanne Dosch, Kathleen Chenoweth-Corby, and Teresa Foelker. Dubuque, IA: Kendall/Hunt Publishing, 1985.

> Explores changes in the American family through interviews with family members. The authors contend that we do not all have to be the traditional family to be valid, viable, functional family units.

FW5. *Child Care and Equal Opportunity for Women.* James A. Levine. Washington, DC: U.S. Commission on Civil Rights, 1981.

> Examines the relationship between the federal government's child care programs and policies and the federal goal of equal opportunity for women.

FW6. *Child Care Fact Sheet.* Washington, DC: National Commission on Working Women, n.d.

> Gives statistics on working mothers and children. Order from 2000 P St., NW, Suite 508, Washington, DC 20036.

FW7. *The Crisis of the Working Mother.* Barbara J. Berg. New York: Summit Books, 1986.

Considers the conflict women experience between family and work. Order from Simon and Schuster Building, 1230 Avenue of the Americas, New York, NY 10020.

FW8. *The Employed Parent.* Jeanie MacDonough, Florence Cherry, and Christian Dean. Ithaca, NY: Cornell Distribution Center, 1984.

Provides parents who are employed or seeking employment with insight into themselves as individuals and family members and with skills that will increase their abilities as responsible parents and workers. Includes facilitator's manual, *Communication for Empowerment* handbook, *Family Matters* film discussion guides, and fact sheets for a nine-session workshop series. Order from 7 Research Park, Ithaca, NY 14850.

FW9. "Executive Etiquette." Jean Nathan. *Tampa Tribune Times*, 23 Mar. 1986.

Highlights changes in rules of etiquette in all kinds of work settings.

FW10. "Executive Women Find It Difficult to Balance Demands of Job, Home." Helen Rogan. *Wall Street Journal*, 30 Oct. 1984, 33.

Emphasizes major physical and emotional strains of female executives with home responsibilities.

FW11. "Expectant Moms, Office Dilemma." Beth Brophy. *U.S. News and World Report*, 10 Mar. 1986, 52–53.

Reports on the impact at the office when pregnant workers are part of the staff.

FW12. *Families at Work: The Jobs and the Pay.* Washington, DC: U.S. Department of Labor, 1984.

Discusses historical trends and changes in labor force and earnings patterns among workers in families. Order from U.S. Department of Labor, Bureau of Labor Statistics, Washington, DC 20212.

FW13. "Good News for Working Women." Jane Bryant Quinn. *Woman's Day*, 4 Mar. 1986, 20.

Shows statistically that although women still earn less than men, as women acquire training, their average pay goes up.

Women with the same skills, education, and experience as men are earning much closer to a man's wage.

FW14. "How Bosses Justify Less Pay for Women." Robert Pear. *State Journal-Register*, 30 Aug. 1985, 15.

Discusses how employers are able to justify paying women less than men.

FW15. "How Working Women Have Changed America." *Working Woman*, Nov. 1986, 129–77.

Contains a series of articles appearing in a special tenth anniversary issue of *Working Woman* magazine. Considers business and economy, law and public policy, the family, housing, marketing, entrepreneurship, and what the future holds.

FW16. *Joblessness among Women: A Portrait of Female Unemployment*. Washington, DC: Coalition on Women and Employment and the Full Employment Action Council, 1985.

Reports on unemployment among women. Order from 815 16th St., NW, Washington, DC 20006.

FW17. *Leave Policies for Adoptive Parents*. New York: Catalyst, 1986.

Considers the growing need for policies that address leaves of absence for adoptive parents. Order from 250 Park Ave. South, New York, NY 10003.

FW18. *Managing Sexual Tension in the Workplace*. New York: Catalyst, 1986.

Discusses how gut-level feelings about gender roles in the home and the workplace can raise barriers that impede women's productivity and advancement and can create uncertainty and discomfort in men. Discusses the use of gender awareness exercises. Order from 250 Park Ave. South, New York, NY 10003.

FW19. "Many Women Decide They Want Their Careers Rather Than Children." Trish Hall. *Wall Street Journal*, 10 Oct. 1984, 35.

Reports on career women without children.

FW20. "More Family Issues Surface at Bargaining Tables as Women Show Increasing Interest in Unions." Cathy Trost. *Wall Street Journal*, 2 Dec. 1986, 66.

> Discusses the unions' increased interest in family-related issues.

FW21. *Moving Ahead on Child Care.* New York: Catalyst, 1985.

> Considers how companies can help employees to balance work and family commitments. Order from 250 Park Ave. South, New York, NY 10003.

FW22. *The Myth of the Working Mother.* Barbara Wallston and Michelle Citron. Pittsburgh, PA: Know, n.d.

> Discusses the myth that when a woman works she is not fulfilling her primary function of keeping house for her husband and caring for her babies. Order from P.O. Box 86031, Pittsburgh, PA 15221.

FW23. "The 1984 Working Woman Report on Money Management." Bonnie Siverd. *Working Woman*, Nov. 1984, 119–22.

> Reveals results of a survey of the saving and investment habits of 900 *Working Woman* readers. Includes a section on the differences of those with and without children.

FW24. *Not as Far as You Think: The Realities of Working Women.* Lynda L. Moore. Lexington, MA: D.C. Heath and Company, 1986.

> Addresses the problems women still face in the workplace and offers some organizational and personal solutions to the gap between myth and reality.

FW25. *On-Site Child Care—Pros and Cons.* New York: Catalyst, 1985.

> Describes the basic benefits and drawbacks of on-site child care. Order from 250 Park Ave. South, New York, NY 10003.

FW26. "The Parental-Leave Debate." Barbara Kantrowitz. *Newsweek*, 17 Feb. 1986, 64.

Reviews the various points of view concerning parental leave policies.

FW27. "The Perk of the Eighties." Robin Micheli. *Working Woman*, June 1986, 132–33.
Discusses child care issues that affect companies.

FW28. *The Photo Album: His Career vs. Our Career.* Corena Mook. Slide presentation/audio tape. Topeka, KS: Division of Community Colleges and Vocational Education, 1985.
Explores dual-career families and shared responsibilities for the household. Order from Vocational Equity, 120 E. 10th St., Topeka, KS 66612.

FW29. *Places in the System: New Directions for the Vocational Education of Rural Women.* Faith Dunne. Paper. Columbus, OH: Ohio State University, 1985.
Discusses the changes in the American culture and in the perception of women's roles that have altered the impact of work on rural women and on their home and family role, and addresses the new needs for vocational preparation and job structures that the changes have generated. Order from Center for Education and Training for Employment, 1900 Kenny Rd., Columbus, OH 43210.

FW30. "Productivity: Families, Work, and the Economy." *J. C. Penney Forum*, May 1983.
Covers such topics as "How Do We Value Work?" "Productivity and the Quality of Life," "Motivators and Satisfiers," "Dual Earner Families," and "Human Factors." Also available is a set of lessons that help educators introduce the concepts in *Forum* magazine and develop in their learners a greater understanding of what productivity means to the individual, the family, and society. Order from J.C. Penney Consumer Education Services, 1301 Avenue of the Americas, New York, NY 10019.

FW31. *The Reality of the Working Force Today.* Corena Mook. Slide presentation/audiotape. Topeka, KS: Division of Community Colleges and Vocational Education, 1985.
Investigates a variety of issues related to the role of women in the work force. Includes preinventory software for Apple

computers. Order from Vocational Equity, 120 E. 10th St., Topeka, KS 66612.

FW32. *The Sexes at Work.* Lois B. Hart and J. David Dalke. Boulder, CO: Leadership Dynamics, 1983.

> Outlines 12 problem areas between men and women and offers concrete solutions for eliminating them. Order from 3775 Iris Ave., Suite 3B, Boulder, CO 80301.

FW33. "Single Parents Who Raise Children Feel Stretched Thin by Home, Job." Betsy Morris. *Wall Street Journal*, 28 Sept. 1984, 27.

> Outlines the pressures of working single parents.

FW34. *Time of Change: 1983 Handbook on Women Workers.* Lenora Cole Alexander. Washington, DC: U.S. Department of Labor, 1983.

> Documents statistically changes in the role of women in the labor force and in the nation's economy. Provides accounting for legal developments. Order from U.S. Department of Labor, Office of the Secretary, Women's Bureau, 200 Constitution Ave., NW, Washington, DC 20210.

FW35. "The Two Lives of a Working Mother." Barbara Berg. *New Woman*, Oct. 1986, 53–54.

> Tells how to turn the drawbacks of being a working mother into assets. Drawn from *The Crisis of the Working Mother* (FW).

FW36. "What If We All Quit Work: The View from 1996." Marvin Schwein. *Working Mother*, Apr. 1986.

> Provides an overview of futuristic prophesies. Includes a series of articles, such as "Five Women Imagine Life Without Their Paycheck," by Linda Lee Small. Considers what the economy and life in America would be like if all women quit their jobs today.

FW37. "Where Do Families Matter?" Patricia Schroeder. *National Business Woman*, Aug./Sept. 1986, 6–7.

> Discusses Sweden as a leader in parental leave policies and other profamily work issues. Includes statistics on other countries and shows where the U.S. stands in relation to other countries.

FW38. *Women and Work.* Pasadena, CA: New Sage, 1986. Profiles 85 women from all walks of life and backgrounds who live in the U.S. and work in a wide variety of jobs. Order from P.O. Box 41029, Pasadena, CA 91104.

FW39. "Women at Work." Karen Pennar and Edward Mervosh. *Business Week*, 28 Jan. 1985.
> Includes a series of articles, such as "Why Can't a Woman's Pay Be More like A Man's" (D) and "The Feminization of Poverty: More Women Are Getting Poorer" (WS).

FW40. *Women at Work: A Chartbook.* Washington, DC: U.S. Department of Labor, 1983.
> Focuses on women's economic activity, including labor force trends, occupational and industrial employment patterns, unemployment, and the market force of women in a family context. Order from U.S. Department of Labor, Bureau of Labor Statistics, Washington, DC 20212.

FW41. "Women at Work: Meeting the Challenge of Job and Family." Carolyn J. Jacobson. *AFL-CIO American Federalist*, 5 Apr. 1986.
> Considers such issues as pay equity, job safety, and union representation for women.

FW42. *Women at Work: Overcoming the Obstacles.* Marlene Arthur Pinkstaff and Anna Bell Wilkinson. Reading, MA: Addison-Wesley, 1979.
> Addresses the problems unique to women in business and industry and offers techniques for overcoming them. Provides information on self-image, family relationships, mentors, ambition, anger, stress, goal setting, support systems, power, politics, sexism, and other related topics.

FW43. *Women's Bureau: Meeting the Challenges of the 80's.* Washington, DC: U.S. Department of Labor, 1985.
> Highlights selected activities and programs that the Women's Bureau has spearheaded to help women in America meet the challenges of the 1980s. Order from U.S. Department of Labor, Office of the Secretary, Women's Bureau, 200 Constitution Ave., NW, Washington, DC 20210.

FW44. "Work and Family." *AFL-CIO American Federalist*, 22 Mar. 1986.

> Contains the text of a statement approved by the AFL-CIO Executive Council that considers issues confronting families today.

FW45. *Work and Family: Walking the Tightrope.* Videocassette. Rockville, MD: BNA Communications, n.d.

> Examines how employers, unions, and governments are responding to the needs of today's workers to walk a tightrope between the demands of their jobs and their family responsibilities. Discusses child care; maternity, paternity, and adoption leave; alternative work schedules; and company-sponsored employee counseling and assistance programs. VHS, 30 min. Order from 9439 Key West Ave., Rockville, MD 20850.

10 Gender Role Stereotyping (GS)

GS1. *Achieving Sex Equity Through Students (ASETS) Training Guide.* Curriculum guide. Wayne, MI: Wayne County Intermediate School District, 1984.

> Includes a two-day training guide for students and teachers, designed to increase their knowledge of the effects of gender role stereotyping on career choice. Male and female student teams, composed of juniors and seniors and assisted by a faculty advisor, lead activities with eighth to tenth graders in their home schools. Presentation activities include value voting, films, checklists, nontraditional worker panels, quizzes, role playing, and analysis of sex bias in the media. Balanced male/female focus. Order from Wayne County Intermediate School District, P.O. Box 807, Wayne, MI 48184.

GS2. *Activities to Raise Student Awareness of Sex Stereotyping Intermediate and Secondary Section.* Harrisburg, PA: Pennsylvania Department of Education, n.d.

> Contains seven activities suitable for junior high and secondary students. Order from 333 Market St., Harrisburg, PA 17126.

GS3. *And Then What Happened?* Filmstrip series. New York: Council on Interracial Books for Children, n.d.

> Develops critical thinking about the behavior of men, women, and children. Encourages children to think about their own behavior. Includes discussion guides. Contains the following filmstrips:
> *Equal Play* (children challenging the lack of gender equity in an after school play center), *Equal Pay* (a working mother's decision to join a strike in an effort to be paid as much as the male workers earn), *Equal Chance* (a teenage girl decides about remaining in an automotive mechanics class despite her boyfriend's disapproval), *Equal Housework* (a single mother and her children decide whether she should marry a man who believes in strict traditional sex roles), and *What*

>   *Kind of Man* (two boys argue about what type of ideal man each prefers—macho versus kind and considerate). For grades K–4. Order from 1841 Broadway, New York, NY 10023.

GS4.   *Another Half.* Videocassette. Austin, TX: Bill Wadsworth Productions, 1986.

>   Helps teenagers, parents, and others become conscious of gender role pressures and traps. Helps teens realize the value of reawakening the important parts of themselves that they have disowned because of gender role expectations. Order from 2404 Rio Grande, Austin, TX 78705.

GS5.   *Are You Hurting Your Daughter Without Knowing It?* Ann Eliasberg. Pittsburgh, PA: Know, n.d.

>   Considers the question "Are you—like many of our schools—teaching your daughter to have fewer aspirations than the boys in her class?" Order from P.O. Box 86031, Pittsburgh, PA 15221.

GS6.   *Aspire: Awareness of Sexual Prejudice is the Responsibility of Educators.* Esther Heusner. Newton, MA: WEEA Publishing Center, 1979.

>   Provides a tool for training teachers to evaluate instructional materials, examine the effects of gender role stereotyping on careers, and develop strategies for lasting change. The four modules—"Sex-role Socialization," "Sexism in Education," "Evaluating Instructional Materials," and "Strategies for Change"—can be used either as individual workshops or as a program series. Order from 55 Chapel St., Suite 200, Newton, MA 02160.

GS7.   "Beginning Equal." *Equal Play Magazine* 3.34 (Summer–Fall 1982).

>   Reports on a project entitled "Beginning Equal: The Project on Nonsexist Childrearing for Infants and Toddlers." The main goal of the project is to help parents and other caregivers of young children raise the next generation so that all children are "beginning equal." Order from Women's Action Alliance, 370 Lexington Ave., New York, NY 10017.

GS8. *Books for Today's Children.* Jeanne Bracken and Sharon Wigutoff. Old Westburg, NY: Feminist, 1979.

> Identifies a list of picture books that avoid stereotyped attitudes and encourage examples of multidimensional characters.

GS9. *Breaking the Chain of Stereotyping.* H. Eugene Wyson. Columbus, OH: Ohio Department of Education, 1986.

> Includes five units on gender role stereotyping and career decision making: stereotyping, influences on future career choices, reasons for employments, peer pressure and decision making, and people in nontraditional careers. For grades 6–12. Order from Sex Equity Stereotyping Unit, Division of Vocational and Career Education, 65 S. Front St., Room 915, Columbus, OH 43266.

GS10. "But Can She Type?" Susan Essick. *National Business Woman*, Feb./Mar. 1986, 21–22.

> Discusses the changing media images of women.

GS11. "Can 'Feminine' Looks Hurt Career Women?" *Newsweek on Campus*, Sept. 1985, 17.

> Points out the pros and cons of looking feminine on the job in this age of change.

GS12. *Career Guidance.* Anne Grant. Videocassette. Newton, MA: WEEA Publishing Center, 1979.

> Considers how gender role stereotyping limits career choices and what counselors and teachers can do about it. Part of *Venture Beyond Stereotypes* program (GS). 3/4 in. Order from 55 Chapel St., Suite 200, Newton, MA 02160.

GS13. "Changing Roles." *Equal Play Magazine* 2.3 (Summer 1981).

> Considers gender role socialization and how to combat it. Order from 370 Lexington Ave., New York, NY 10017.

GS14. *Changing Roles of Men and Women: Educating for Equity in the Workplace.* Margaret A. Nash. Madison, WI: University of Wisconsin, 1991.

> Includes curriculum that can be used in whole or in part in a variety of settings, such as in-services, workshops, class-

rooms, or programs for graduate credit. Subjects include demographics and workforce changes, effects of gender role stereotyping on men and women, occupational segregation, sexual harassment, pay inequity, language barriers, treatment of students, and administrative policies. Order from Center on Education and Work, University of Wisconsin-Madison, Department AM, 1025 W. Johnson St., Madison, WI 53706.

GS15. *Child Care Shapes the Future: Anti-Sexist Strategies.* Filmstrip series. New York: Council on Interracial Books for Children, n.d.

Discusses how our expectations determine treatment of boys and girls and set up role models of boys as aggressive and inquisitive and girls as gentle and docile. Outlines ten anti-sexist child care strategies and gives suggestions to help educators become more sensitive to their role in creating an antisexist environment. For early childhood staff and parents. Order from 1841 Broadway, New York, NY 10023.

GS16. *Comparisons of Female and Male Early Adolescent Sex Role Attitude and Behavior Development.* Christine Nelson and Joanne Keith. Madison, WI: Society for Research on Adolescence, 1986.

Examines the differences between female and male early adolescents in studies that have been previously reported. Focuses on the comparisons between male and female early adolescents in gender role attitude and behavior development. Reports and discusses differences in levels of traditionalism of gender role attitudes and behaviors and differences in significant environments and influences.

GS17. *Competence Is for Everyone.* Martha Whalen Kent, Andrea K. Blanch, Anne M. Woolfson, and Dale Kent. Newton, MA: WEEA Publishing Center, 1978.

Takes a historical look at stereotypes and injustice. Students analyze their appraisals of others and of themselves and scrutinize employment practices, educational institutions, the law, and the media, as they learn critical-thinking skills.

Includes the following units in both intermediate and upper levels: "Different People" (surveys why people make appraisals and what the effects are), "In the Minority" (helps nonminority students empathize with minority group members), "Male and Female" (explores the narrow world of gender-based expectations), "Competence in Our Society" (reviews the basic concept of appraisal and encourages participants to change the way they make judgments about others), and "Gender and the Conditions of Learning: Collected Readings" (shows how youngsters can be pigeonholed by parents and schools). May be used with *The Rise of Rolag* (GS) and/or *Judge Me, Not My Shell* (D) videocassettes. Order from 55 Chapel St., Suite 200, Newton, MA 02160.

GS18. *Consciousness Raising Activities for Use in the Classroom.* Tacoma, WA: School District No. 10, 1978.

Shares 28 activities that can be used in the classroom to raise awareness of equity issues. Order from P.O. Box 1357, Tacoma, WA 98401.

GS19. *Critical Events Shaping Women's Identity: A Handbook for the Helping Professions.* Donna M. Avery. Newton, MA: WEEA Publishing Center, 1980.

Shows how gender role stereotyping can affect helping professionals—male and female—despite their best efforts. Based on interviews with educated women—middle-class and upper-class, African-American and white. Helps counselors and prospective counselors hone sensitivity. Order from 55 Chapel St., Suite 200, Newton, MA 02160.

GS20. *Cultural Values.* Anne Grant. Videocassette. Newton, MA: WEEA Publishing Center, 1979.

Examines the conflicts experienced by young men and women who resist social or family pressure to fill expected roles. Part of *Venture Beyond Stereotypes* program (GS). 3/4 in. Order from 55 Chapel St., Suite 200, Newton, MA 02160.

GS21. "Educating Women: No More Sugar and Spice." Florence Howe. *Saturday Review*, 16 Oct. 1971.

Discusses gender role stereotyping.
GS22. "Eliminating Sex Stereotyping." Sam Stern and Forrest Gathercoal. *School Shop*, Feb. 1984, 17–18.
> Contains suggestions for combating stereotyping in a traditionally stereotyped location—the school shop.

GS23. *An Equal Chance: A Parent's Introduction to Sex Fairness in Vocational Education.* Martha Matthews and Shirley McCune. Pamphlet. Washington, DC: Resource Center on Sex Roles in Education, 1978.
> Discusses ways parents can help children overcome stereotyping and can help schools provide equal opportunity. Stock no. 017-080-01863-2. Order from Superintendent of Documents, Government Printing Office, Washington, DC 20402.

GS24. *Equality in Vocational Programs.* Dorothy Lawrence. Denver, CO: State Board of Community Colleges and Occupational Education, 1979.
> Contains a compilation of articles and resource materials that can be implemented by vocational educators to reduce sex bias and gender role stereotyping in vocational programs. Includes a general reference, an administrative reference, and a counselor's/teacher's handbook. Order from Occupational Education Division, Sex Equity Section, State Board of Community Colleges and Occupational Education, Denver, CO 80201.

GS25. *Expanding Career Options Curriculum Manual.* Joyce Fouts, Jim Mahrt, and Suzanne Lewandowski. Wayne, MI: Wayne County Intermediate School District, 1985.
> Contains a lesson guide designed to create an awareness of gender role stereotyping and career development in general and in the world of work. Provides information to maximize career alternatives for males and females and explores alternatives to traditional work and family roles. Pilot-tested in Michigan schools. Balanced male/female focus. Order from 33500 Van Born Rd., Wayne, MI 48184.

GS26. *Expectations.* Glee Ingram. Videocassette. Newton, MA: WEEA Publishing Center, n.d.

Illustrates subtle forms of gender role stereotyping in daily activities. 3/4 in., 16 min. For use with *Together We Can* training programs (GS). Order from 55 Chapel St., Suite 200, Newton, MA 02160.

GS27. "A Fabulous Child's Story." Lois Gould. *Ms.*, Dec. 1972.

Tells the fictitious story of "Baby X," who was part of a secret scientific experiment where the child was raised as neither a boy nor a girl, but as an "X."

GS28. *Focus of the Future.* Lewis E. Patterson. Newton, MA: WEEA Publishing Center, 1978.

Makes junior high and high school students aware of how people stereotype according to sex and of how such stereotyping limits opportunities. Students respond to a variety of pictures of adults in work and home situations, followed by group discussions that explore student attitudes toward work and family relationships. Includes technical manual, leader's manual, and picture stimulus sets. Order from 55 Chapel St., Suite 200, Newton, MA 02160.

GS29. "A Framework for Sex Role Counseling." Ellen Piel Cook. *Journal of Counseling and Development*, Dec. 1985, 253–58.

Contains a framework for gender role counseling applicable to both sexes and based on the androgyny model of masculinity and femininity.

GS30. *Freeing Ourselves: Removing Internal Barriers to Equality.* Helen V. Collier and Jessie Lovano-Kerr. Newton, MA: WEEA Publishing Center, 1982.

Details a workshop that helps women overcome the psychological barriers of gender role stereotyping. Readings, mini-lectures, and discussion questions lead participants to a critical examination of their attitudes about careers, education, and social identity. Role-playing activities encourage participants to experiment with new behaviors on the spot. Gives step-by-step instructions for setting up a practical program relevant to women of varied ages and professions. Includes a sound filmstrip. Order from 55 Chapel St., Suite 200, Newton, MA 02160.

GS31. "Growing Up Free." *Equal Play Magazine* 1.4 (Fall 1980).

Considers how parents and teachers can contribute to a nonsexist environment for children. Order from 370 Lexington Ave., New York, NY 10017.

GS32. *How Schools Shortchange Girls.* Washington, D.C.: American Association of University Women Educational Foundation and the National Education Association, 1992.

Reports on major findings of a study on girls and education commissioned by the AAUW Educational Foundation and researched by the Wellesley College Center for Research on Women. Challenges the common assumption that girls and boys are treated equally in our public schools. Provides information on gender roles, girls' school experiences from preschool through advanced studies, and test bias; perspectives on curriculum; and recommendations for change. Includes statistics and references. An 8-page summary of the full 116-page report, including the fully stated 40 recommendations for change, is also available. Order from AAUW Sales Office, P.O. Box 251, Annapolis Junction, MD 20701.

GS33. *Humanity as a Career: A Holistic Approach to Sex Equity.* Gary N. McLean and Jacquelyn S. Crawford. Rehoboth, MA: Twin Oaks Publishing, n.d.

Illustrates and examines through a collection of articles the subtle and not-so-subtle influences of sexism that we have grown up and lived with.

GS34. "If 'Good Managers' Are Masculine, What Are 'Bad Managers'?" Gary N. Powell and D. Anthony Butterfield. *Sex Roles* 10.7–8 (1984): 477–84.

Examines the perceived characteristics of bad and good managers. In contrast to stereotypic views of the good manager as masculine, bad managers were seen by business students as low in both masculinity and femininity.

GS35. *I'm Me.* Poster. Brooklyn, NY: TABS Aids for Equal Education, n.d.

Contains a poem on a variety of activities a child can do. Is written by a 12-year-old girl and includes photos of a boy sewing, a girl climbing, a boy and girl dancing, and so on. Includes a note on the writer of the poem and a lesson plan on writing a poem about oneself. Order from 744 Carroll St., Brooklyn, NY 11215.

GS36. "Just How the Sexes Differ." *Newsweek*, 18 May 1981, 72–83.

Considers anthropological differences between men and women and relates findings to sex bias.

GS37. *Law Enforcement Presentation.* Brian S. Surprenant. Slide presentation. Springfield, IL: Illinois State Board of Education, 1986.

Discusses gender role stereotyping in the law enforcement field. Part of the *Sex Equity in Law Enforcement and Corrections* series (R). 42 slides, 13 min. script. Order from Department of Adult, Vocational, and Technical Education, 100 N. First St., Springfield, IL.

GS38. "Learning Sex-Equitable Social Skills." Kathryn P. Scott. *Theory into Practice* 25.4 (Autumn 1986): 243–49.

Focuses on positive social skills in which there is a disparity between the performance of females and males, including leadership, self-confidence, emotional sensitivity, empathy, and prosocial behaviors.

GS39. *The Masculine Mystique.* Anne Grant. Videocassette. Newton, MA: WEEA Publishing Center, 1979.

Provides a lively reminder that sex bias works both ways. Part of the *Venture Beyond Stereotypes* program (GS). 3/4 in. Order from 55 Chapel St., Suite 200, Newton, MA 02160.

GS40. *Men and Women: After the Revolution.* Videocassette. Fred Simon. Boston, MA: Fanlight Productions, 1984.

Features interviews with 12 men and women—some single, some married, divorced, or remarried—who talk openly about what it is like to try to be "grown up" in a time of ever-changing gender roles. VHS, 56 min., black and white. Order from 47 Halifax St., Boston, MA 02130.

GS41. *People and Places, U.S.A.* Miriam Weiss. Newton, MA: WEEA Publishing Center, 1981.
> Reports on three boys and three girls spending several summers traveling together around the U.S. Sharing the exciting adventures of these fictional characters helps students develop a positive self-image and encourages them to shed stereotyped attitudes about gender and career roles. Includes teacher's guide. Order from 55 Chapel St., Suite 200, Newton, MA 02160.

GS42. *Programs for Parents.* Toni F. Clark and Pamela M. Wilson. Washington, DC: Center for Population Options, 1983.
> Describes several successful programs designed to train parents to be the sexuality educators of their children and lists the steps necessary for setting up a new program. Order from 2301 Florida Ave., NW, Washington, DC 20009.

GS43. *Programs to Combat Stereotyping in Career Choice.* Palo Alto, CA: American Institutes for Research, 1980.
> Describes several programs that were developed to combat gender role stereotyping in career choice. Order from P.O. Box 1113, Palo Alto, CA 94302.

GS44. *The Report Card 1: The Cost of Sex Bias in Schools.* Myra Sadker and David Sadker. Washington, DC: Mid-Atlantic Center for Sex Equity, 1981.
> Highlights several findings related to sex differences and sex discrimination in school. Order from 5010 Wisconsin Ave., NW, Suite 308, Washington, DC 20016.

GS45. *The Report Card 2: Sex Bias in Colleges and Universities.* Myra Sadker. Washington, DC: Mid-Atlantic Center for Sex Equity, 1984.
> Summarizes research and draws a profile of what is happening to women in colleges and universities. Offers information on faculty, students, curriculum, and instruction. Order from 5010 Wisconsin Ave., NW, Suite 308, Washington, DC 20016.

GS46. *The Report Card 6: Gifted Girls—The Disappearing Act.* Susan Morris Shaffner. Washington, DC: Mid-Atlantic Center for Sex Equity, 1986.

> Discusses factors contributing to the "disappearing act" of gifted girls. Considers how society limits gifted girls, how gifted girls limit themselves, and how to help gifted girls achieve. Order from 5010 Wisconsin Ave., NW, Suite 308, Washington, DC 20016.

GS47. *Reverse Sex Stereotyping—Case in Point: Court Reporting.* Beverly Stitt and Marcia Anderson. Springfield, IL: Illinois State Board of Education, 1978.

> Analyzes the phenomenon of male gender role stereotyping in vocational education, more specifically court reporting in Illinois. The problem of the study was to determine to what extent gender role stereotyping may be a barrier to the recruitment of male students in court reporting education. Funded by the Department of Adult, Vocational, and Technical Education. Order from 100 N. First St., Springfield, IL 62777.

GS48. *The Rise of Rolag.* Martha Whalen Kent. Videocassette. Newton, MA: WEEA Publishing Center, 1977.

> Gives elementary students a unique introduction to stereotyping. Rolag becomes a victim of stereotyping because of the shape of his head. Includes script, discussion questions, and teacher's worksheet. 15 min. For use with the *Competence Is for Everyone* series (GS). Order from 55 Chapel St., Suite 200, Newton, MA 02160.

GS49. "The School Experiences of Black Girls: The Interaction of Gender, Race, and Socioeconomic Status." Diane Scott-Jones and Maxine L. Clark. *Phi Delta Kappan*, Mar. 1986, 520–26.

> Examines the combined effects of gender, race, and socioeconomic variables on African-American girls. Part of the "Women in Education" series (T).

GS50. *Sex Stereotyping in Education.* Patricia Campbell. Newton, MA: WEEA Publishing Center, 1987.

Helps weed out the gender role stereotyping that infects the classroom in a comprehensive staff-training program. Thirteen modules highlight the achievements and contributions of women; each module includes an audiotape cassette, a bibliography, an instruction sheet, and handouts. The modules include "Girl, Boy, or Person," "Sex Stereotyping in Math Doesn't Add Up," "Equality in Science," "Present but Not Accounted For," "Reading, Writing, and Stereotyping," "We the People," "Exercising Your Rights," "Repainting the Sexist Picture," "Business as Usual," "A New Beginning," "Diagnosing the Problem," "Write Me In," and "Sex Bias in Research and Measurement." Funded by the Women's Educational Equity Act. Order from 55 Chapel St., Suite 200, Newton, MA 02160.

GS51. *A Tall Tale.* Poster. New York: TABS Aids for Equal Education, n.d.

Tells about supergirl Lynn Jones, who solves her town's population problems. Written and illustrated by two nine-year-old girls. Includes a lesson plan on sex roles in folktales. Order from 744 Carroll St., Brooklyn, NY 11215.

GS52. *Thinking and Doing: Overcoming Sex-Role Stereotyping in Education.* Dorothy Stein et al. Newton, MA: WEEA Publishing Center, 1978.

Includes a guide to career guidance, curriculum design, and student activities. Order from 55 Chapel St., Suite 200, Newton, MA 02160.

GS53. *Today's Changing Roles: An Approach to Non-Sexist Teaching.* Resource Center on Sex Roles in Education. Washington, DC: National Foundation for the Improvement of Education, 1974.

Contains supplemental instructional materials that can be used to assist children to explore and understand the ways that gender role stereotypes have defined and limited male and female roles. Order from Suite 918, 1156 15th St., NW, Washington, DC 20005.

GS54. *Together We Can—Community Training Kit.* Glee Ingram. Newton, MA: WEEA Publishing Center, 1979.

Helps ally the school and the community in the effort to eradicate gender stereotyping and create the environment students need to become bias-free adults. Includes a program guide; the facilitator's manual for community groups, school volunteers, and parents; and participants' manual masters for parent, community, and volunteer groups. The videocassette *Expectations* (GS) is a helpful training film for use with this kit. Order from 55 Chapel St., Suite 200, Newton, MA 02160.

GS55. *Together We Can—Elementary and Secondary Training Kit.* Glee Ingram. Newton, MA: WEEA Publishing Center, 1979.

Helps ally the school and the community in the effort to eradicate gender role stereotyping and create the environment students need to become bias-free adults. Includes a facilitator's manual and participants' manual masters for teachers and counselors and for school administrators. Includes three filmstrips with audiotape cassettes: *Which Comes First—The Person or the Role, Images and Our Self-Concept,* and *Stop, Look, Listen.* Also includes five transparencies, game cards, and articles. The videocassette *Expectations* (GS) is a helpful training film for use with this kit. Order from 55 Chapel St., Suite 200, Newton, MA 02160.

GS56. *Understanding Institutional Sexism.* Filmstrip. New York: Council on Interracial Books for Children, 1982.

Helps viewers understand that sexism is so ingrained in our basic social structures that changes will require revision not only of individual attitudes and behaviors but of institutional policies and practices that produce sexist results. Order from 1841 Broadway, New York, NY 10023.

GS57. *Understanding Sex Roles and Moving Beyond.* Joanna Allman et al. Newton, MA: WEEA Publishing Center, 1979.

Discusses gender roles in American society, stereotyping, and strategies for moving beyond the stereotypes. Part of the *Female Experience in America* package (WS). Order from 55 Chapel St., Suite 200, Newton, MA 02160.

GS58. *Venture Beyond Stereotypes.* Anne Grant. 8 videocassette series. Newton, MA: WEEA Publishing Center, 1979.
> Explores how cultural patterns and values affect us. Helps teachers show youngsters the facts and the feelings behind them. The workbook, *Venture Beyond Stereotypes: A Workbook for Teachers Concerned about Sex-Role Stereotyping,* outlines eight two-hour sessions of activities and lively discussions. Videocassette titles are *Classroom Practices* (T); *Early Childhood* and *Athletics and Physical Education* (I); *The Masculine Mystique, Career Guidance,* and *Cultural Values* (GS); and *The Feminist Mystique* and *Language and Textbooks.* Order from 55 Chapel St., Suite 200, Newton, MA 02160.

GS59. *We Are Woman.* Filmstrip. Studio City, CA: Motivational Media, 1986.
> Contains an upbeat look at the issues men and women confront today. Narrated by Helen Reddy. Provides a statistical base on males and females in the paid work force and the changing values of today's society. 30 min., 16 mm. Order from 11429 Dona Pegita Dr., Studio City, CA 91604.

GS60. *Why Jenny Can't Lead.* Jinx Melia and Pauline Lyttle. Grand Junction, CO: Operational Politics, 1986.
> Explains the "male dominant system" and decodes the differences between men's and women's perceptions of their roles and responsibilities. Unravels the mysteries of power strategies in America. Order from P.O Box 9173, Grand Junction, CO 81501.

GS61. *Woman and Man.* Videocassette. Princeton, NJ: Films for the Humanities, 1988.
> Considers the differences between men and women. Phil Donahue speaks with men and women in many walks of life. 52 min. Order from P.O. Box 2053, Princeton, NJ 08543.

GS62. *Women in Sports.* Poster. New York: TABS Aids for Equal Education, n.d.
> Depicts women engaged in sports. Includes a lesson plan on the benefits of sports. Order from 744 Carroll St., Brooklyn, NY 11215.

GS63. *Women Seen on Television.* Jennifer Sass. Videocassette. Portland, OR: Letting Go Foundation, 1990.

Presents a lively video and study guide that promote awareness and stimulate discussion. The video blends narration, clips of broadcast footage of advertising and program content, and rock music into a fast-paced, critical look at television's stereotypical view of women. For grade 6–adult. Order from 02000 S.W. Palatine Hill Rd., Portland, OR 97219.

GS64. "Working Toward Equity: Cribs to Classrooms." *Graduate Women,* Jan./Feb. 1987.

Considers gender equity issues in a series of articles.

GS65. "Workplace Remains Sex-Segregated, Panel Concludes." Anne Bridgman. *Education Week,* 8 Jan. 1986, 10.

Reveals findings of a two-year study conducted by a committee of the National Research Council, a branch of the National Academy of Sciences.

11

History (H)

H1. *American Women: Making History.* Laura Burges. Play script. Santa Rosa, CA: National Women's History Project, 1986.

>Extends to children an appreciation of American women throughout history. For grades 5–12. Can be done simply, as a classroom activity, or can be expanded with the use of costumes and props. Order from P.O. Box 3716, Santa Rosa, CA 95402.

H2. *Her Way.* Mary-Ellen Kulkin. Chicago, IL: American Library Association, 1976.

>Includes a collection of 260 short profiles and bibliographies of notable women throughout history and an additional bibliography of over 300 collective biographies of women.

H3. *In Search of Our Past: Units in Women's History.* Susan Groves. Newton, MA: WEEA Publishing Center, 1980.

>Recounts the history of unsung women—ordinary and extraordinary—in American and world history. Engaging and informative essays, stories, and activities not only enlighten students but enable them to gain a strong sense of their own connection to the past. Includes teacher's and students' manuals for American and world history units. Order from 55 Chapel St., Suite 200, Newton, MA 02160.

H4. *Integrating Women into U.S. History: A Sourcebook.* Part I, *Women in the 18th and 19th Centuries.* Sheila Culbert and Jane E. Gastineau. Bloomington, IN: Indiana University, 1983.

>Contains a series of lessons aimed at supplementing the limited material dealing with women's history normally found in junior and senior high school American history textbooks. Companion to Part 2, *Women in the 20th Century.*

H5. *Integrating Women into U.S. History: A Sourcebook.* Part 2, *Women in the 20th Century.* Sheila Culbert and Jane E. Gastineau. Bloomington, IN: Indiana University, 1983.

>Contains a series of lessons aimed at supplementing the limited material dealing with women's history normally

found in junior and senior high school American history textbooks. Companion to Part 1, *Women in the 18th and 19th Centuries.*

H6. *My Name Is Lucretia Mott.* Poster. New York: TABS Aids for Equal Education, n.d.

Depicts a child dressed as Lucretia Mott in a classroom dramatization. Poster text is Mott's biography in a child's words. Includes a lesson plan for a classroom "Living Biography" project. Order from 744 Carroll St., Brooklyn, NY 11215.

H7. *National Women's Hall of Fame Coloring Book.* Carole Stallone. Santa Rosa, CA: National Women's History Project, 1982.

Contains line drawings of 15 women from the National Women's Hall of Fame and a two-line biographical statement for each woman. Order from P.O. Box 3716, Santa Rosa, CA 95402.

H8. *National Women's History Week Community Organizing Guide.* Santa Rosa, CA: National Women's History Project, 1985.

Provides a wide variety of activities that celebrate National Women's History Week, including sample letters, fliers, and news releases. Order from P.O. Box 3716, Santa Rosa, CA 95402.

H9. *Notable Black Women.* Nancy Ellin. Lansing, MI: Michigan Department of Education, 1984.

Provides material for teachers and students interested in learning more about the lives and achievements of famous African-American women. Contains 24 biographical sketches, five activities or games that teachers can tear out and reproduce, writing assignments, and several hands-on and artistic activities. For junior high and up. Order from P.O. Box 30008, Lansing, MI 48909.

H10. *101 Wonderful Ways to Celebrate Women's History.* Bonnie Eisenbert and Mary Ruthsdotter. Santa Rosa, CA: National Women's History Project, 1986.

Includes activities that can be implemented by the school system alone, by the school system and the community cooperatively, and by individuals or community-based organizations. Order from 7738 Bell Rd., Windsor, CA 95492.

H11. *Remember the Ladies!* Robin Franklin and Tasha Lebow Wolf. Ann Arbor, MI: University of Michigan, 1980.

Includes writings in handbook format of or about women from various eras in American history, including the years between 1600 and the present. For high school and up. Order from Center for Sex Equity in Schools, 1046 School of Education, Ann Arbor, MI 48109.

H12. *Stereotypes, Distortion, and Omissions in U.S. History Textbooks.* New York: The Council on Interracial Books for Children, 1977.

Examines history textbooks for sex and race fairness. Order from Racism and Sexism Resource Center for Educators, 1841 Broadway, New York, NY 10023.

H13. *Susan B. Anthony Coin.* Poster. Brooklyn, NY: TABS Aids for Equal Education, n.d.

States "Money Talks . . . About America." Depicts three coins and the ideals symbolized on them (penny/Lincoln/emancipation; quarter/Washington/liberty; dollar/Anthony/equality). Includes a lesson plan on the American ideals featured on the coins. Order from 744 Carroll St., Brooklyn, NY 11215.

H14. *Trivial Perusal.* Game. Santa Rosa, CA: National Women's History Project, 1985.

Contains 726 questions. Has rules, but will fit the commercially popular trivia game format. Includes world women, historic women, Minnesota women (8 percent), and contemporary women. A Minnesota Women's Consortium activity. For high school to adult. Order from P.O. Box 3716, Santa Rosa, CA 95402.

H15. *Women Have Always Worked.* Alice Kessler-Harris. New York: Feminist, 1981.

Explores the history of the working lives of women in the
U.S. from the colonial period to the present. Order from
Box 334, Old Westbury, NY 11568.
H16. *Women in History.* Computer software. Santa Rosa,
CA: National Women's History Project, 1986.
Provides clues for students to identify 34 prominent women
in the world from the last two centuries. The program is
designed for whole-class use and permits students to com-
pete for the right answer. Includes teacher's guide. For
grades 6–11. Order from P.O. Box 3716, Santa Rosa, CA
95402.
H17. *Women of Achievement.* Poster set. TABS Aids for Equal
Education, n.d.
Features a diverse group of famous and less well-known
women. Set of 24 posters. Each includes a biography. Order
from 744 Carroll St., Brooklyn, NY 11215.
H18. *Women of Ideas (And What Men Have Done to Them).*
Dale Spender. Santa Rosa, CA: National Women's History
Project, 1983.
Includes over 50 biographies of women living in the past
300 years. Order from P.O. Box 3716, Santa Rosa, CA
95402.
H19. *Women's History Week: March 6–12.* Charles D.
Moody. Ann Arbor, MI: University of Michigan, 1982.
Contains a collection of lesson plans regarding women in
history. The lessons are designed to be adaptable to various
age groups and group sizes and to serve as alternative lesson
plans. Order from Center for Sex Equity in Schools, Ann
Arbor, MI 48109.

12 Home Economics (HE)

HE1. "Beyond Gender: Equity Issues for Home Economics Education." Patricia J. Thompson. *Theory Into Practice* 25.4 (Autumn 1986): 226–83.

> Discusses equity issues as they relate to home economics education.

HE2. "The Class Where Fairytales Are Left Behind." Yvonne Ferguson and Martha Lee Blankenship. *VocEd*, Apr. 1980.

> Describes the "Adult Roles and Functions" course taught in West Virginia public high schools.

HE3. *Excellence in Parenthood/Child Development Education.* Gene Bottoms. Arlington, VA: American Vocational Association, 1984.

> Identifies exemplary parenthood/child development education programs as models for adoption or adaptation nationwide. Program presentations and nomination abstracts are included. Order from 1410 King St., Arlington, VA 22314.

HE4. *Home Economics Unlimited.* Doris Dopkin. New Brunswick, NJ: Rutgers University, 1978.

> Describes home economics programs that provide meaningful learning experiences for students, regardless of gender. Order from New Brunswick, NJ 08903.

HE5. *A Just Beginning: Sex Equity Manual for Childbirth Educators.* Patricia Mitchell Corsi, William C. Lloyd, Jr., and Mel Madden. Newton, MA: WEEA Publishing Center, 1981.

> Provides parents-to-be who participate in this workshop the opportunity to learn to recognize their sex biases and to begin parenthood with positive feelings about their sexuality and gender roles. Order from 55 Chapel St., Suite 200, Newton, MA 02160.

HE6. *Making Home Economics Relevant to Males.* Camille G. Bell and Gloria E. Durr. Austin, TX: Texas Education Agency, 1980.

> Provides guidelines for meeting and coping with the problems perceived by male students enrolled in vocational home-

making programs. Order from Texas Education Agency, Department of Occupational Education and Technology, Research Coordination Unit, Austin, TX 78710.

HE7. "Sex Equity in Parenting and Parent Education." Diane Scott-Jones and Wilma Peebles-Wilkins. *Theory Into Practice* 25.4 (Autumn 1986): 235–42.

Examines gender equity and related equity issues, such as race and class, in parenting and parent education.

HE8. "Teen Parents: The Crisis and the Challenge for Vocational Education." Karen Pittman. *Workplace Education*, May/June 1986, 8–9.

Discusses methods for convincing teens to delay parenthood.

13 In-service Training (I)

I1. *Athletics and Physical Education.* Anne Grant. Videocassette. Newton, MA: WEEA Publishing Center, 1979.
Shows what some schools have done to achieve great results with coeducational sports programs. Part of the *Venture Beyond Stereotypes* program (GS). Order from 55 Chapel St., Suite 200, Newton, MA 02160.

I2. *Becoming Sex Fair: The Tredyffrin/Easttown Program— A Comprehensive Model for Public School Districts.* Marilyn E. Calabrese. Newton, MA: WEEA Publishing Center, 1979.
Provides systemwide help in selecting, developing, applying, and evaluating techniques for improving sex fairness in schools. Includes *Coordinator's Manual, Stage One Manual: Preparing for Change, Stage Two Manual: Planning the In-service Program,* and *Stage Three Manual: Revising the Curriculum.* Order from 55 Chapel St., Suite 200, Newton, MA 02160.

I3. *A Better Way.* Rich Feller. Videocassette. Fort Collins, CO: Colorado State University, 1986.
Demonstrates how nontraditional adults and those with special needs can access vocational education and transition from school to employment and further training. Includes guidebook for conducting an in-service program. Order from School of Occupational and Educational Studies, Colorado State University, Fort Collins, CO 80523.

I4. *Beyond the Bake Sale.* Anne R. Henderson, Carl L. Marburger, and Theodora Ooms. Columbia, MD: National Committee for Citizens in Education, 1986.
Provides an educator's guide to working with parents and achieving parent involvement. Order from Suite 410, Wilde Lake Village Green, Columbia, MD 21044.

I5. *Building Sex Equity in Vocational Education: An In-service Training Program.* Shirley McCune and Martha Matthews. Washington, DC: National Foundation for the Improvement of Education, 1980.

Outlines four 90-minute in-service training sessions designed to increase vocational educators' capability to achieve gender equity in vocational education. Includes facilitator's handbooks and participants' workbooks. Discusses the social/educational perspective, the legal perspective, and methods for building individual skills and vocational programs. Order from 1201 16th St., NW, Washington, DC 20036.

I6. *Building Your Own Scenario.* Louise Vetter, Rodney K. Spain, and Maureen E. Kelly. Columbus, OH: National Center for Research in Vocational Education, 1981.

Helps vocational service area leaders infuse the concepts and practices of gender equity through training programs in home economics, trade and industry, business and office occupations, technical education, industrial arts, health occupations, agriculture, and marketing and distributive education. Includes facilitator's guides. Order from Center on Education and Training for Employment, 1900 Kenny Rd., Columbus, OH 43210.

I7. *The Career Shopper's Guide: A Development Plan Manual for an Employment Resource and Training Service.* Gerri Hair. Newton, MA: WEEA Publishing Center, 1980.

Provides a practical guide for workshop planning that treats the job search as a function of a woman's needs and talents. Included are workshops that focus on the special concerns of African-American and Latina/Hispanic women, information for teachers of technical or trade courses, and tips for family members adjusting to a mother working outside the home. Order from 55 Chapel St., Suite 200, Newton, MA 02160.

I8. *Changing Roles of Men and Women: Implications for Vocational Education.* Mary Thompson. Curriculum guide. Madison, WI: Wisconsin Board of Vocational, Technical, and Adult Education, 1984.

Contains materials of a course taught in late 1983 to instructors, counselors, and administrators in Wisconsin. Order from 4802 Sheboygan Ave., P.O. Box 7874, Madison, WI 53707.

I9.   *Curriculum and Research for Equity (CARE): A Training Manual for Promoting Sex Equity in the Classroom.* Marlaine E. Lockheed, Karen J. Finkelstein, and Abigail M. Harris. Newton, MA: WEEA Publishing Center, 1982.

Presents an elementary school teacher training program that ferrets out causes of gender role stereotyping in the individual, the classroom, and the school. Six two-hour sessions of activities, analyses, and discussions sensitize staff and faculty to intrusive gender role stereotyping and enable them to remedy it. The workshops consider men and women in society, language and behavior, female leadership, and other issues. Order from 55 Chapel St., Suite 200, Newton, MA 02160.

I10.   *Early Childhood.* Anne Grant. Videocassette. Newton, MA: WEEA Publishing Center, 1979.

Presents ways to set up nonsexist classrooms and community, religious, and recreational centers for the full development of all young children. Part of the *Venture Beyond Stereotypes* program (GS). Order from 55 Chapel St., Suite 200, Newton, MA 02160.

I11.   *Equity Training for State Education Agency Staff.* Washington, DC: Resource Center on Educational Equity, 1986.

Provides a status report for state education agency (SEA) equity staff on federal and state roles in promoting educational equity; an overview of inequities based on race, sex, national origin, and disability that continue to exist in our educational system; and an encouragement for equity staff to cooperatively integrate equity concerns into SEA programs and activities. Order from Council of Chief State School Officers, 400 N. Capitol St., NW, Suite 379, Washington, DC 20001.

I12.   *Expanding Career Options Participant Guide.* Joyce Fouts, Jim Mahrt, and Suzanne Lewandowski. Wayne, MI: Network Project, 1986.

Contains a two-day training guide for teachers, counselors, and administrators that is designed to increase awareness of the effects of sex bias and gender role stereotyping on males and females. Enables participants to plan activities that combat the negative effects of sex bias on students' career choices through awareness training for school staff, tested classroom activities to explore sex bias, review of career and guidance materials for sex bias, and identification and utilization of nontraditional role models. Pilot-tested in Michigan. Balanced male/female focus. *Expanding Career Options Counselor Workshop* (CG) and *Expanding Career Options Curriculum Manual* (GS) also available. Order from Wayne County Intermediate School District, 33500 Van Born Rd., Wayne, MI 48184.

113. *Expanding Options.* Lynn Stuve. Newton, MA: WEEA Publishing Center, 1984.

Presents a series of awareness, knowledge, and action-planning workshops on sexism and gender role stereotyping. Provides a coordinator's guide with all the information needed to coordinate separate workshops for eight different groups in the educational community and facilitator's guides with step-by-step instructions and the necessary minilectures, activity guides, and transparency masters for each group workshop. Includes workshop guides for elementary teachers, secondary teachers, counselors, administrators, parents, student leaders, students, and support staff. Order from 55 Chapel St., Suite 200, Newton, MA 02160.

114. *Exploring Educational Equity: Sex-Affirmative Guide for Counseling and Teaching.* Patricia G. Ball et al. Newton, MA: WEEA Publishing Center, 1981.

Contains teaching and learning guides for courses in education, psychology, social work, medicine, counseling, and career education. Includes effective lesson plans, activities, and resource materials that explore new techniques for counseling women, sex bias in measuring career interest, women in higher education, affirmative action in education, and assertiveness training for job seekers. Individual units are written for the teacher or group leader, who can then relay sex-fair, sex-affirmative attitudes and teaching or counseling techniques to classroom participants. Order from 55 Chapel St., Suite 200, Newton, MA 02160.

115. *Freedom for Individual Development.* Barbara F. Powers. Newton, MA: WEEA Publishing Center, 1978.

Provides an in-service training program designed to illuminate teachers' attitudes. Each module contains instructions for a group trainer, activities for group work, background readings, evaluation tools, and a resource bibliography. Modules include "School/Community Relations," "Vocational Education," "Teaching Methods and Instructional Materials," and "Counseling and Guidance." Order from 55 Chapel St., Suite 200, Newton, MA 02160.

116. *The Gifted Girl: Helping Her Be the Best She Can Be.* Linda Addison. Bethesda, MD: Equity Institute, 1983.

Contains techniques by which those who interact with gifted or bright girls can remove subtle roadblocks that might prevent the girls from achieving their maximum potential. Individual manuals for teachers, community youth group leaders, parents, and counselors and an in-service resource handbook that includes seven workshop formats are available. Order from P.O. Box 30245, Bethesda, MD 20814.

117. *Implementing Title IX and Attaining Sex Equity: A Workshop Package for Postsecondary Educators.* Martha Matthews and Shirley McCune. Washington, DC: U.S. Government Printing Office, 1980.

Includes modules designed for use by persons implementing training or staff development efforts for education personnel and interested citizens in the implementation of Title IX and the attainment of gender equity in postsecondary institutions. Contains the modules "Content of Title IX," "Implications of Title IX for Postsecondary Physical Education and Athletic Personnel," "Planning for Change: The Teacher Educator's Role, the Counselor's Role, and the Administrator's Role," and a participant notebook. Order from Superintendent of Documents, 725 N. Capitol St., NW, Washington, DC 20402.

118. *New Pioneers.* Amanda J. Smith. Newton, MA: WEEA Publishing Center, 1980.

> Makes staff aware of the subtle ways sexism can creep into the curriculum, into teacher expectations, and into student thinking. For K–12. Includes seminar leader's handbook. Successful program in North Carolina. Order from 55 Chapel St., Suite 200, Newton, MA 02160.

119. *Promoting Educational Equity Through School Libraries.* Allen Pace Nilsen and Karen Beyard Tyler. Newton, MA: WEEA Publishing Center, 1978.

> Tells librarians, teachers, and administrators everything they need to know about selecting and cataloging sex-fair materials, finding alternative references, and taking advantage of community resources. Each of the five modules—"Assumptions about 'Male' and 'Female'," "Sexism and Sex-Role Stereotyping in School Materials," "Sex-Fair Instructional Materials," "Sex-Fair Resources for School Libraries," and "Educational Equity in the Library"—can be presented as a short workshop. Order from 55 Chapel St., Suite 200, Newton, MA 02160.

120. *Recommended Resources for Use in Developing Programs to Achieve Sex Equity in Mathematics, Science, and Technology.* Mary Jo Strauss. Baltimore, MD: Maryland State Department of Education, 1987.

> Lists materials that help overcome the problem of low female interest in science and technical careers. Lists materials for trainer in-service programs and materials for student readings. Order from Division of Vocational-Technical Education, Maryland State Department of Education, Baltimore, MD 21201.

121. *Sex Equity Awareness Activities.* Warren Hall. Springfield, IL: Illinois State Board of Education, 1978.

> Contains 12 activities that help individuals explore the issue of gender equity. Order from Department of Adult, Vocational, and Technical Education, 100 N. First St., Springfield, IL 62777.

122. *Sexism in Schools.* Norma T. Mertz and Susan C. Companiotta. Knoxville, TN: Educational Media Center, 1980.

> Includes a comprehensive package of materials designed to assist those involved in decision making for elementary/secondary education. Includes a slide/audio tape show that describes what sexism in schools is, a guide for making a school visit to determine if sexism exists, a videotape (3/4 in., 30 min.) of gender equity related situations the viewer must resolve, and a guide for assessing and eliminating sexism in a school district. Order from 305 Claxton Building, University of Tennessee, Knoxville, TN 37966.

123. *Teacher Skill Guide for Combatting Sexism.* Debra Klinman. Newton, MA: WEEA Publishing Center, 1979.

> Provides a quick, simple tool for pinpointing subtle examples of sex bias in teachers' lessons and in students' attitudes. Contains activities, background readings, and handouts for workshop leaders. Phase 1 includes "How Expectations Influence Behavior and Perception," "Sex Bias in Language and Instructional Materials," "Dealing with Resistance to Change," "Developing New Classroom Structures That Require Role Flexibility," and "Fostering Independence." Phase 2 includes "The Components of a Nonsexist Person," "Teaching the Components of a Nonsexist Person," and "Using the Role Play to Develop the Behaviors of a Nonsexist Person." Phase 3 includes "Problem Solving Around Personal Issues Related to Sex Bias," "Developing Internal Strength Through Self-Statements," "Helping Students Build Internal Strength," "Helping Students Identify with Role Models," and "Developing the Components of a Nonsexist Person Through Guided Daydreams." Order from 55 Chapel St., Suite 200, Newton, MA 02160.

124. *Title IX—Administrators: Implementing Sex Equity.* Martha Matthews and Shirley McCune. Denver, CO: Department of Education, 1980.

> Consists of a Title IX/Sex Equity training model designed to help educational personnel and interested citizens implement

Title IX. For elementary and secondary school administrators. Includes trainer's and participants' manuals.

I25. *Title IX—Athletics: Achieving Sex Equity.* Martha Matthews and Shirley McCune. Denver, CO: Colorado Department of Education, 1979.

Consists of a Title IX/Sex Equity training model designed to help educational personnel and interested citizens implement Title IX. Intended for physical educators, coaches, athletic directors, and related administrators. Includes trainer's and participants' manuals.

I26. *Title IX—Physical Education: Implementing Sex Equity.* Martha Matthews and Shirley McCune. Denver, CO: Department of Education, 1979.

Consists of Title IX/Sex Equity training model designed to help educational personnel and interested citizens implement Title IX. Intended for physical educators, coaches, and related administrators of local education agencies. Includes trainer's and participants' manuals.

I27. Title IX—Planning for Change: Title IX and Sex Equity. Martha Matthews and Shirley McCune. Denver, CO: Department of Education, 1980.

Consists of Title IX/Sex Equity training model designed to help educational personnel and interested citizens implement Title IX. Intended for local staff, including administration, Title IX coordinators, instructional staff, counselors and student personnel, vocational education personnel, physical education and athletics staff, board members, and representatives of community groups. Includes trainer's and participants' manuals.

I28. *Title IX—The Community's Role: Implementing Title IX and Sex Equity.* Martha Matthews and Shirley McCune. Denver, CO: Department of Education, 1980.

Consists of Title IX/Sex Equity training model designed to help educational personnel and interested citizens implement Title IX. Intended for community groups, parents, and others not employed by the school district. Includes trainer's manual.

129. *Together We Can—Preschool Training Kit.* Glee Ingram. Newton, MA: WEEA Publishing Center, 1979.

Helps ally the school and the community in the effort to eradicate gender role stereotyping and create the environment students need to become bias-free adults. Includes a program guide, the facilitator's manual for preschool educators and parents of preschool children, a participants' manual master for educators and parents of preschool children, a pocket chart and cards, game boards and cards, the filmstrip *Evaluating the Classroom Environment*, and seven transparencies. The videocassette *Expectations* (GS) is a helpful training film for use with this kit. Order from 55 Chapel St., Suite 200, Newton, MA 02160.

14
Legislation (L)

L1. *Citizens Council on Women Annual Report.* Citizens Council on Women. Springfield, IL: Illinois Citizens Assembly, 1986.

> Details the areas of public policy addressed by the council since its inception in the spring of 1986 and the council's specific recommendations to the Illinois General Assembly. Published annually. Order from 300 W. Monroe, Springfield, IL 62706.

L2. *Destination . . . Sex Fair Education.* Terri Reed. Harrisburg, PA: Pennsylvania Department of Education, 1980.

> Designed to be a student's introduction to Title IX legislation. Order from Publications, Pennsylvania Department of Education, 11th Floor, P.O. Box 911, 333 Market St., Harrisburg, PA 17108.

L3. *Equal Education under Law.* Rosemary C. Salomone. New York: St. Martin's, 1986.

> Provides a detailed history of legal rights in American education and addresses issues of equal educational opportunity for racial and linguistic minorities, the handicapped, and women.

L4. *Equity from a Business, Industry, and Labor Perspective.* Irving Kovarsky. R and D Series no. 214P. Columbus, OH: National Center for Research in Vocational Education, 1982.

> Traces legislative developments favorably or unfavorably affecting employment equity. Order from Center on Education and Training for Employment, 1900 Kenny Rd., Columbus, OH 43210.

L5. *Equity from a Legal Perspective.* Lisa Aversa Richette. R and D Series no. 214K. Columbus, OH: National Center for Research in Vocational Education, 1982.

> Defines equity as justice and fairness and traces the history of its development through law and court cases related to equity for women. Order from Center on Education and

Training for Employment, 1900 Kenny Rd., Columbus, OH 43210.

L6.   *Illinois Women* 1.1 (Spring 1987). Illinois Citizens Assembly, Citizens Council on Women.

Provides the council's membership, legislative agenda, and annual report, and discusses the impact of the state budget on women and children. Published annually.

L7.   *It's Not Funny/It's Illegal: A Handbook of Laws Guaranteeing Equal Education and Employment Opportunities.* Susan Ripley. Quincy, MA: Massachusetts Department of Education, 1981.

Familiarizes students with the general laws that guarantee them protection. Funded through the Division of Occupational Education.

L8.   *Legislative Update: Parental Leave.* Pamphlet. New York: Catalyst, 1987.

Discusses the legislative and corporate climate regarding the issue of parental leave. Order from 250 Park Ave. South, New York, NY 10003.

L9.   *Rights on the Job.* Videocassette. Columbus, OH: Ohio Department of Education, 1986.

Discusses the history and evolution of employment laws. Part of a series on Equal Employment Opportunity Legislation. Funded through the Division of Vocational and Career Education. VHS, 12 min., color.

L10.   *Sex Bias: Education Legislation and Regulations.* Grace L. Mastalli. Washington, DC: National Advisory Council on Women's Educational Programs, 1977.

Highlights seven federal programs aimed at creating educational equity for women. Order from 1832 M St., NW, Washington, DC 20036.

L11.   "Sex with Professors." Claudia Driefus. *Glamour*, Aug. 1986.

Discusses ways to handle sexual harassment in college classrooms.

L12.   *Sexual Harassment.* Bonnie Eisenberg. Santa Rosa, CA: Sonoma County Commission on the Status of Women, n.d.

Provides general information about sexual harassment and legal rights under federal and state law. Order from 370 A Administration Dr., Santa Rosa, CA 95401.

L13. *The State-by-State Guide to Women's Legal Rights.* NOW Legal Defense and Education Fund and Renee Cherow-O'Leary. New York: McGraw Hill, 1987.

Provides an up-to-date guide to the laws in the 1980s affecting women's lives in the areas of home and family, education, employment, and the community.

L14. *Title IX Grievance Procedures: An Introductory Manual.* Martha Matthews and Shirley McCune. Washington, DC: National Foundation for the Improvement of Education, 1976.

Discusses the basics of grievance procedures, evaluating or developing a Title IX grievance procedure while considering both internal and external factors, administering the grievance procedure, and the role of the Title IX coordinator. Order from 1201 16th St., NW, Washington, DC 20056.

L15. *Title IX: The Regulation and the Grievance Process.* Martha Matthews and Shirley McCune. Denver, CO: Department of Education, 1979.

Consists of a Title IX/Sex Equity training model designed to help education personnel and interested citizens implement Title IX. Includes trainer's and participants' workbooks. For local education agency staff—including administrators, Title IX coordinators, instructional staff, counselors and student personnel workers, vocational education personnel, and physical education and athletics staff—and for board members and representatives of community groups.

L16. *Tune In to Your Rights* . . . Barbara Morris et al. Ann Arbor, MI: Center for Sex Equity in Schools, 1985.

Contains a guide for teenagers about sexual harassment. Order from Center for Sex Equity in Schools, 1046 School of Education Building, University of Michigan, Ann Arbor, MI 48109.

L17. *Violence Against Women.* Catherine Walters. Springfield, IL: Illinois Coalition Against Domestic Violence, 1984.

Contains information about sexual assault, domestic violence, and the victims of these crimes. Order from 931 S. Fourth St., Springfield, IL 62703.

L18.   *Who's Hurt and Who's Liable.* Curriculum guide. Quincy, MA: Massachusetts Department of Education, 1983.
Provides curriculum for sexual harassment in secondary schools. Developed for all members of the school community. Defines sexual harassment, explains the legal issues involved, describes administrative strategies, and presents student activities and classroom lessons. Order from 1385 Hancock St., Quincy, MA 02169.

L19.   "Women's Rights Cases May Show Where the Court is Headed." Paula Dwyer. *Business Week*, Oct. 1986, 55–56.
Considers several issues of women's rights that were decided in the Supreme Court in the 1986–87 term.

15 Male Focus (M)

M1. *Andrew.* Videocassette. Long Beach, CA: Southerby Productions, n.d.

> Tells the delightful story of a young boy who decides to become a nurse, to his father's dismay and his classmates' amusement. Presents a new understanding of sex roles and communication between parent and child. VHS, 1/2 in. 24 min. Order from P.O. Box 15403, Long Beach, CA 90815.

M2. *As Boys Become Men: Learning New Male Roles.* Doug Thompson. Denver, CO: University of Colorado at Denver, 1980.

> Considers the restrictions imposed by the male role stereotype. Contains classroom activities. Order from Institute for Equality in Education, 1050 Ninth St., Denver, CO 80202.

M3. *Being a Man.* Cathleen M. O'Toole, ed. Columbus, OH: Ohio State University, 1980.

> Helps students, parents, and educators understand the context in which gender role stereotyping and sex discrimination may affect men. Includes discussion questions, classroom activities, transparency masters, and bibliography. Order from Ohio Distributive Education Materials Laboratory, 123 Townshend Hall, 1885 Neil Ave., Columbus, OH 43210.

M4. *Being a Man, in a Man's World, Doing Manly Things, Alongside of and with Other Men.* Robert A. Zuckerman. Columbus, OH: Ohio State University, 1980.

> Considers through simulation various avenues men's lives may take. Order from Ohio Distributive Education Materials Lab, 123 Townshend Hall, 1885 Neil Ave., Columbus, OH 43210.

M5. *Boy and Doll.* Poster. Brooklyn, NY: TABS Aids for Equal Education, n.d.

> Depicts boy holding and feeding a doll, with the heading "He may be a father someday" and the verses of the song "William's Doll." Includes lesson and activity sheet. Order from 744 Carroll St., Brooklyn, NY 11215.

M6. *Challenges: A Young Man's Journal for Self Awareness and Personal Planning.* Mindy Bingham, Judy Edmondson, and Sandy Stryker. El Toro, CA: Mission Publications, 1985.
> Addresses the problems teenage boys and girls encounter as they move toward adulthood. Designed to help students think about the future, set goals, clarify values, make sound decisions, assert themselves, and evaluate career choices. Companion to *Choices: A Teen Women's Journal for Self Awareness and Personal Planning* (CG). Instructor's guide and students' workbook available. Order from P.O. Box 25, El Toro, CA 92630.

M7. "Changing Men, Changing Marriage." W. M. Meade. *Working Woman*, Nov. 1986.
> Describes the male view of how marriage has changed as a result of women having their own careers.

M8. *Counseling Men.* Thomas M. Skovholt, Paul G. Schauble, and Richard Davis, eds. Belmont, CA: Wadsworth, 1980.
> Provides counselors and psychotherapists with useful information, concepts, and strategies regarding the behavior of males.

M9. "Husbands Who Star in Supporting Roles." Denie S. Weil. *Working Woman*, June 1986, 114–16.
> Discusses the phenomenon of husbands taking a career detour to give their wives a chance to move ahead in their professions.

M10. "Male Stereotyping Isn't Fair." Beverly Stitt. *VocEd*, Nov.–Dec. 1988, 12–14.
> Reviews some of the stereotyped behavior stamping that men learn as children, which can result in poor performance in school, career disatisfaction, and poor health.

M11. *Men in Dual-Career Families.* Lucia Albina Gilbert. Hillsdale, NJ: Lawrence Erlbaum Associates, 1985.
> Reports on an investigation of men in dual-career families and considers interventions at the societal and individual level that will ease the difficulties associated with the transition to this family form.

M12. "My Male Sex Role—and Ours." Joseph Peck. *Win*, 11 Apr. 1974, 8–12.
> Describes a man's perspective on the traditional male role.

M13. *New Relations.* Ben Achtenbert. Videocassette. Boston, MA: Fanlight Productions, 1980.
> Explores the economic and emotional costs and rewards of the filmmaker's decision to become a father in his mid-thirties and of his choice to share child care responsibilities equally with his wife. Filmed as the filmmaker's son approached his first birthday. VHS, 34 min. Order from 47 Halifax St., Boston, MA 02130.

M14. "A New Vision of Masculinity." D. Cooper Thompson. *Educational Leadership*, Dec. 1985–Jan. 1986, 53–56.
> Examines and challenges traditional male roles.

M15. *On Being Father.* Frank Ferrara. Garden City, NY: Doubleday, 1985.
> Expresses a divorced man's views about sharing the responsibilities of parenthood.

M16. *Programs for Young Men.* Douglas Beckstein, Marjorie B. Dahlin, and Dinah Wiley. Washington, DC: Center for Population Options, 1983.
> Describes several sexuality education programs for adolescent males and outlines guidelines for setting up a new program. Includes resource listing. Order from 2031 Florida Ave., NW, Washington, DC 20009.

M17. *The Relationship Between Father Involvement and Sex-Role Development among Late Adolescents.* Michael R. Stevenson. Paper presented at the meeting of the Society for Research on Adolescence, Madison, Wisconsin, Mar. 1986.
> Investigates the relationship between aspects of father involvement as perceived by sons and daughters and gender role self-concept among late adolescents. Results show that more masculine females were closer to their fathers than those who were less masculine, androgynous females had the best relationships with their fathers, and masculine males were closer to their fathers than nonmasculine males. Partici-

pants living with their father perceived him as a better parent
than did those not residing with him. Order from the Department of Psychological Science, Ball State University,
Muncie, IN 47306.

M18.   *Single Fathers.* Geoffrey L. Greif. Lexington, MA: Lexington Books, 1985.

Analyzes the myths and realities regarding single fathers who
are raising their children following a divorce. Order from
D.C. Heath and Company, Lexington Books, Lexington,
MA 02173.

M19.   *Stale Roles and Tight Buns: Images of Men in Advertising.*
Michael Markovitz. Videocassette. Boston, MA: 1988.

Uses common advertising images to show how the media stereotypes men. Focuses on the myths used to define and limit
the American man. Examines the definition of "real men" and
encourages critical thinking about the pressures that shape the
ideal man. Topics include cowboys and heroes, money and
power, men and emotions, military images, violence, isolation
and competition, muscles and sexuality, romance and women,
and fathering. Order from Illinois State Curriculum Center,
Sangamon State University, Springfield, IL 62794.

M20.   "Superdads." Maureen Hayden. *Evansville Courier and
Press,* 9 Mar. 1986, Evansville, IN.

Interviews fathers regarding their hopes for their children
and indicates a change from traditional goals.

M21.   *Ties That Bind: The Price of Pursuing the Male Mystique.*
Washington, DC: Project in Equal Education Rights, 1981.

Considers the toll that gender role stereotyping has taken
on men. Includes examples of limitations men contend with
to achieve cultural masculinity. Order from 1413 K St., NW,
9th Floor, Washington, DC 20005.

M22.   " 'Women's Liberation' Aims to Free Men, Too." Gloria Steinem. *Washington Post,* 7 June 1970.

States that men are limited when women are limited and
that freedom for women results in new freedoms for men.

16 Math and Science (MS)

MS1. *Add-Ventures for Girls.* Margaret Franklin. 2 vols. Reno, NV: University of Nevada, 1990.

Contains hands-on activities to expose elementary and junior high school girls to the exciting world of math. Builds on the latest research to provide the tools teachers need to make math relevant to elementary and junior high girls. Order from WEEA Publishing Center, 55 Chapel St., Suite 200, Newton, MA 02160.

MS2. *American Women in Science Biographies.* Mary Ellen Verheyden-Hilliard. Bethesda, MD: Equity Institute, 1985.

Contains 10 biographies of contemporary American women scientists from diverse racial and ethnic groups. Easy-to-read text for elementary students. Includes the videocassette *You Can Be A Scientist, Too!* (VHS, 13 min.) which shows children that their "why" and "what if" questions are the same kinds of questions scientists ask and that childhood activities can lead to future careers. Includes teacher's guides. Order from P.O. Box 30245, Bethesda, MD 20814.

MS3. *Beating the Numbers: A Woman's Math Careers Program Handbook.* Ferol Breymann. Newton, MA: WEEA Publishing Center, 1980.

Lays out a successful 16-week program for women with a high school diploma or GED who need to overcome math anxiety and learn skills for jobs. May be used for group instruction and one-on-one counseling. Provides activities, a resource list, and a special matrix that pinpoints the math skills needed for various jobs. Order from 55 Chapel St., Suite 200, Newton, MA 02160.

MS4. *Breakthrough: Women in Science.* Diana C. Gleasner. Santa Rosa, CA: National Women's History Project, 1984.

Profiles the lives of six women scientists to inspire young women interested in science careers. Order from P.O. Box 3716, Santa Rosa, CA 95402.

MS5. *Count Me In: Educating Women for Science and Math.* Lenore Blum. Videocassette. Newton, MA: WEEA Publishing Center, 1978.

>Outlines how the Women in Science program at Mills College in Oakland, California, led to a dramatic increase in student enrollment in math and computer science courses. Includes brochure. Designed for science classes and career workshops. Order from 55 Chapel St., Suite 200, Newton, MA 02160.

MS6. *The Double Bind: The Price of Being a Minority Woman in Science.* Shirley Mahaley Malcom, Paula Quick Hall, and Janet Welsh Brown. Washington, DC: American Association for the Advancement of Science, 1976.

>Reports on the Conference of Minority Women Scientists held in Airlie House, Warrenton, Virginia, Dec. 1975. Order from 1515 Massachusetts Ave., NW, Washington, DC 20005.

MS7. *Dropping Math? Say Good-Bye to 82 Jobs.* Poster. Toronto, ON: Toronto Board of Education, n.d.

>Depicts a bull's-eye with four concentric circles, each listing jobs requiring math. Order from Mathematics Department, 155 College St., Toronto, Ontario M5T 1P6.

MS8. *Encouraging Girls in Math and Science.* Patricia B. Campbell. 4 Pamphlets. Groton, MA: Campbell-Kibler Associates, 1992.

>Translates the latest findings on girls in math and science into practical suggestions and easy steps for concrete action. For parents, educators, and trainers. Includes "Working Together;" "Making Changes;" "Math, Science, and Your Daughter;" "Nothing Can Stop Us Now;" and "What Works and What Doesn't?" Order from WEEA Publishing Center, 55 Chapel St., Suite 200, Newton, MA 02160.

MS9. *Equity and Excellence: Compatible Goals.* Shirley M. Malcom. Washington, DC: American Association for the Advancement of Science, 1984.

>Assesses programs that facilitate increased access and achievement of females and minorities in K–12 mathematics

and science education. Order from Office of Opportunities in Science, 1776 Massachusetts Ave., NW, Washington, DC 20036.

MS10. *Expanding Your Horizons in Science and Mathematics.* Joanne Koltnow. Newton, MA: WEEA Publishing Center, 1980.

Encourages young women to consider careers in science and technology and directs teachers and parents on how to plan, conduct, and evaluate conferences for young women. May be used in conjunction with the videocassettes *The Math-Science Connection: Educating Young Women for Today* and *Sandra, Zella, Dee, and Claire: Four Women in Science* (MS). Order from 55 Chapel St., Suite 200, Newton, MA 02160.

MS11. *Fair Play: Developing Self-Concept and Decision-Making Skills in the Middle School (Decisions about Math).* Byron G. Massialas. Newton, MA: WEEA Publishing Center, 1983.

Explores occupational aspirations and expectations and decision-making skills in a program of mathematics. Includes teacher's and students' guides. Implementation handbook available. Order from 55 Chapel St., Suite 200, Newton, MA 02160.

MS12. *Futures Unlimited I: Expanding Your Horizons in Mathematics and Science.* Videocassette. New Brunswick, NJ: State University of New Jersey, 1986.

Provides role models of women who have pursued careers in fields related to math and science. Encourages young women to study math and science in high school. 29 min. Order from Consortium for Educational Equity, Rutgers, Kilmer Campus 4090, New Brunswick, NJ 08903.

MS13. *How High the Sky? How Far the Moon? An Educational Program for Girls and Women in Math and Science.* Sharon L. Menard. Newton, MA: WEEA Publishing Center, 1979.

Shows how to teach science and equity at the same time. Includes an annotated list of materials for each grade and a four-audiotape cassette series entitled *Women Scientists Today*. Order from 55 Chapel St., Suite 200, Newton, MA 02160.

MS14. *How to Encourage Girls in Math and Science.* Joan Skolnick, Carol Langbort, and Lucille Day. Englewood Cliffs, NJ: Prentice-Hall, 1982.

> Explains how teachers and parents can help girls develop the skills and confidence to pursue a full range of interests and careers in math and science. Reveals how gender role socialization influences a child's skill development and attitudes toward learning. Provides specific strategies and activities that can be used to improve girls' problem-solving skills and build trust in their intellectual abilities. For grades K–8. Order from Route 9-W, Englewood Cliffs, NJ 07632.

MS15. *Math Report.* Milford, MI: Michigan Project on Equal Education Rights, 1982.

> Reports on the status of math education in Michigan in 1981–82. Considers overall enrollments and the gender gap. Includes recommendations and listing of resources. Order from 211 E. Commerce, Milford, MI 48042.

MS16. *Math: Who Needs It?* Toronto, Ontario: Toronto Board of Education, 1983.

> Includes a resource booklet intended for secondary education students. Cartoons answer students' questions concerning career choices and the usefulness of math. Order from Math Department, 155 College St., Toronto, Ontario M5T 1P6.

MS17. *Mathco.* Carole Hall Hardeman. Newton, MA: WEEA Publishing Center, 1982.

> Reduces math anxiety by helping girls feel competent about their ability to work with numbers. Modules currently available are module 1, "Math and Careers" (includes teacher's guide and sound filmstrip), and module 5, "Math and Science" (includes teacher's guide and the sound filmstrip *MATHCO's Magic Squares*). Modules include in-service manuals. Order from 55 Chapel St., Suite 200, Newton, MA 02160.

MS18. *Mathematics: A Key to the Future.* Toronto, Ontario: Toronto Board of Education, 1981.

Provides parents or guardians key career information. Order from Mathematics Department, 155 College St., Toronto, Ontario M5T 1P6.

MS19. *Mathematics and the Teacher.* Toronto, Ontario: Toronto Board of Education, 1981.

Provides teachers or parents the highlights of the *Mathematics: The Invisible Filter* report (MS). Order from Mathematics Department, 155 College St., Toronto, Ontario M5T 1P6.

MS20. "The Mathematics Filter." Sheila Tobias. *National Forum*, Fall 1981, 17–18.

Indicates that one barrier to women in the professions, lack of study of math-related subjects, may be cured.

MS21. *Mathematics: The Invisible Filter.* Toronto, Ontario: Toronto Board of Education, 1983.

Includes a complete report on math avoidance, math anxiety, and career choices. Order from Mathematics Department, 155 College St., Toronto, Ontario M5T 1P6.

MS22. *Mathophobia Can Cost You a Career.* Poster. Toronto, Ontario: Toronto Board of Education, n.d.

Lists vocational choices unavailable to people with a fear of math. Order from Mathematics Department, 155 College St., Toronto, Ontario M5T 1P6.

MS23. *The Math-Science Connection: Educating Young Women for Today.* Lenore Blum. Videocassette. Newton, MA: WEEA Publishing Center, 1980.

Presents four exemplary programs for girls and women considering scientific or technical study. Meant for use with *Expanding Your Horizons in Science and Mathematics* handbook (MS). Order from 55 Chapel St., Suite 200, Newton MA 02160.

MS24. *Nothing but Options.* Videocassette. Oakland, CA: Mills College, n.d.

Interviews five young career women in math- and science-based jobs about how and why they entered the fields of environmental science, computer graphics, computer systems management, electrical engineering, and financial investments. 17 min. Order from Math/Science Network, 2727 College Ave., Berkeley, CA 94705.

MS25. *Programs in Science, Mathematics, and Engineering for Women in the United States, 1966–1978.* Michele L. Aldrich and Paula Quick Hall. Washington, DC: American Association for the Advancement of Science, 1980.

> Describes over 300 projects designed to increase the numbers and status of women in science, engineering, and mathematics training and careers. Order from Office of Opportunities in Science, 1776 Massachusetts Ave., NW, Washington, DC.

MS26. *Sandra, Zella, Dee, and Claire: Four Women in Science.* Lenore Blum. Videocassette. Newton, MA: WEEA Publishing Center, 1980.

> Looks at the scientific careers of four women—an astronomer, a veterinarian, a laser physicist, and an engineer. Meant for use with *Expanding Your Horizons in Science and Mathematics* handbook (MS). Order from 55 Chapel St., Suite 200, Newton, MA 02160.

MS27. *Science EQUALS Success.* Catherine R. Conwell. Charlotte, NC: Charlotte-Mecklenburg School System, 1990.

> Contains over thirty hands-on discovery-oriented science activities designed especially for girls and students of color, grades 4–9. Incorporates four processes identified by the nationally recognized EQUALS Program as particularly successful with or needed by this special population: problem solving, cooperative learning, spatial skills, and career awareness. Order from WEEA Publishing Center, 55 Chapel St., Suite 200, Newton, MA 02160.

MS28. *Science, Sex, and Society.* Ann E. Kammer, Cherlyn S. Granrose, and Jan B. Sloan. Newton, MA: WEEA Publishing Center, 1979.

> Examines through an anthology the education of women in science, science as a career, and the sometimes competing interests of family and profession. Includes sketches of notable women scientists, such as astronomer Maria Mitchell.

The extensive bibliographies and career counseling resources help science teachers design an introductory course to encourage young women to explore opportunities in science. Order from 55 Chapel St., Suite 200, Newton, MA 02160.

MS29. *Scientific Careers for Women: Doors to the Future.* Videocassette. Ann Arbor, MI: The University of Michigan, n.d.

Addresses the barriers that discourage young women from entering science-related careers. Compilation of the *Women in Science* videotape series (MS). Order from Women in Science Videotape Series, B322 School of Dentistry, University of Michigan, Ann Arbor, MI 48109.

MS30. *The Sky's the Limit in Math-Related Careers.* Judy Askew. Newton, MA: WEEA Publishing Center, 1982.

Educates students about careers in math and science. Women who work in computer science, engineering, finance, and other math-related fields offer anecdotes, points of view, and inside information that convey their determination and sense of fulfillment. An appendix lists professional organizations ready to supply additional help and information. Order from 55 Chapel St., Suite 200, Newton, MA 02160.

MS31. *Snakes Have Bad Manners.* Poster. New York: TABS Aids for Equal Education, n.d.

Depicts a girl holding a snake. Text consists of facts about snakes. Order from 744 Carroll St., Brooklyn, NY 11215.

MS32. *Survive and Succeed in Math.* Toronto, Ontario: Toronto Board of Education, 1983.

Uses an advice column and cartoon format to provide suggestions to students for dealing with math anxiety and study skills. For grades 6–10. Order from Mathematics Department, 155 College St., Toronto, Ontario M5T 1P6.

MS33. *Teacher Education and Mathematics (TEAM).* Elaine B. Chapline and Claire M. Newman. Newton, MA: WEEA Publishing Center, 1984.

Enables prospective teachers to reduce their own anxiety level about math, to develop solid math-teaching skills, and to create a positive classroom environment that avoids gender role stereotyping. Can form the basis for teacher education courses or can be used as supplements. Includes an instructor's handbook and the following modules: "Patterns, Approximation, and Estimation"; "Metric Measurement"; "Choice and Chance"; "Demystifying Math"; "Sex-Role Stereotyping in Mathematics Education"; "Women, Mathematics, and Careers"; and "Women as Mathematicians." Order from 55 Chapel St., Suite 200, Newton, MA 02160.

MS34. *What Will Happen . . . Young Children and the Scientific Method.* Barbara Sprung. Washington, DC: U.S. Department of Education, 1985.

Describes activities that foster early math and science skills, help children understand technology in the world around them, and ensure that all children participate. Order from Educational Equity Concepts, 114 E. 32nd St., New York, NY 10016.

MS35. "What's a Nice Girl Like You Doing in a Math Class?" Patricia B. Campbell. *Phi Delta Kappan*, Mar. 1986, 516–20.

Reviews the evidence that treating groups of students differently and with differing expectations has an impact on achievement. Suggests effective means of counteracting problems. Part of the "Women in Education" series (T).

MS36. *A Winning Formula.* Videocassette. New York: New York City Board of Education, n.d.

Motivates elementary school students, especially girls, to pursue interest in mathematics and science. Portrays the diverse lives, interests, and studies of six young female recipients of the Westinghouse Science Talent Search Award. Includes a program guide that contains articles describing the issues of gender equity in the study of math and science, sample lesson plans and activities, and lists of human and print resources. For grades 4–7. May be shown to parents and teachers to raise awareness. Order from 110 Livingston, Room 625, Brooklyn, NY 11201.

MS37. *Women in Science.* Videotape series. Ann Arbor, MI: University of Michigan, 1986.

Contains seven videotapes that encourage young women to take courses in science and mathematics and to consider careers in biomedicine, chemistry, computer science, dentistry, engineering, geology, and physics/astronomy. VHS, 1/2 in., 30 min. each. Order from Women in Science Videotape Series, B322 School of Dentistry, University of Michigan, Ann Arbor, MI 48109.

MS38. *Women, Math, and Science: A Resource Manual.* Ann Arbor, MI: University of Michigan, 1984.

Compiles resources for encouraging girls in math and science. Order from Center for Sex Equity in Schools, 1046 School of Education, University of Michigan, Ann Arbor, MI 48109.

MS39. *Women, Numbers, and Dreams.* Teri Hoch Perl and Joan M. Manning. Windsor, CA: National Women's History Project, 1982.

Includes math puzzles, activities, and illustrations accompanying 13 biographical sketches of women mathematicians. Includes teacher's manual. For grades 3–6. Order from 7738 Bell Rd., Windsor, CA 95492.

MS40. "Women's Work." Vera Rubin. *Science*, July/Aug. 1986, 58–65.

Considers the barriers that face women in science careers.

MS41. *Your Child and Mathematics: Interest and Encouragement Can Make a Difference.* Toronto, Ontario: Toronto Board of Education, 1983.

Provides career and labor force information and answers questions frequently raised by parents. Based on the findings of the report *Mathematics: The Invisible Filter* (MS). Order from Mathematics Department, 155 College St., Toronto, Ontario M5T 1P6.

17 Nontraditional Careers (NT)

NT1. *Acceptance and Adjustment of People in Nontraditional Occupations.* Lucy Campbell-Thrane and Wesley E. Budke. *VocEd*, Apr. 1980, 10–12.

Considers barriers and problems people face in training for and working in nontraditional occupations.

NT2. *Alternatives: A Guide to Training for Non-Traditional Careers in Southern Nevada.* Joyce Nelson-Leaf. Henderson, NV: Clark County Community College, 1987.

Helps men and women choose careers based on their interests and abilities rather than on gender role expectations. Lists training programs available in Las Vegas, Nevada. Order from Sex Equity Awareness Project, Henderson, NV 89015.

NT3. *Anything You Want to Be.* Parsipany, NJ: American Telephone and Telegraph, 1976.

Employs values-clarification techniques to help students evaluate preferences and personal priorities in social and vocational options. Encourages consideration of nontraditional careers by providing models of people who have found fulfillment in these areas. Develops an awareness of how male/female roles and behavior patterns are formed. Presents a clear picture of the changes in the job market and the effect they can have on individual options, and provides information about legislation and executive orders that have increased job opportunities for all. Designed for use on the secondary level in social studies, family living, English, science, psychology, and career education curricula. Includes leader's discussion guide and transparency/spirit masters.

NT4. *Asian-American Women Today.* Poster. Brooklyn, NY: TABS Aids for Equal Education, n.d.

Depicts a filmmaker, welder, musician, engineer, and taxi driver, with a quote by each. Includes a lesson plan on Asian-American women and interviews with the five women featured on the poster. Order from 744 Carroll St., Brooklyn, NY 11215.

NT5. "Barriers and Detours on Her Career Path." Gail Fullerton. *National Forum*, Fall 1981, 7–8.

Considers the obstacles facing women as they pursue a career in educational administration.

NT6. "Blue-Collar Jobs for Women." Muriel Lederer. *National Forum*, Fall 1981, 20–21.

Discusses the chances for and obstacles to success for women who hold traditionally male blue-collar jobs.

NT7. "Breaking Through: Women on the Move." *U.S. News and World Report*, 29 Nov. 29, 1982.

Discusses how women are steadily toppling barriers and assuming leadership in fields that have traditionally been closed to them.

NT8. *Breakthrough: Women in Archaeology*. Barbara Williams. Santa Rosa, CA: National Women's History Project, 1981.

Considers archaeology as a career and profiles the lives of six contemporary women of diverse backgrounds now working as archaeologists. Order from P.O. Box 3716, Santa Rosa, CA 95402.

NT9. *Breakthrough: Women in Law*. Betsey Covington Smith. Santa Rosa, CA: National Women's History Project, 1984.

Profiles six successful women lawyers, including Sandra Day O'Connor. Order from P.O. Box 3716, Santa Rosa, CA 95402.

NT10. *Careers*. Poster set. New York: TABS Aids for Equal Education, n.d.

Challenges job stereotypes by depicting females and males in nontraditional careers. Includes eight posters and lessons. Order from 744 Carroll St., Brooklyn, NY 11215.

NT11. *The Choice of a Lifetime*. Videocassette. Springfield, IL: Illinois State Board of Education, 1987.

Interviews women and men working in careers not traditional for their sex. For junior high and up. 3/4 in., 26 min.

Order from Illinois State Curriculum Center, Sangamon State University, Springfield, IL 62794.

NT12. *Choices, Challenges, and Changes.* Videocassette. Springfield, IL: Illinois State Board of Education, 1986.
> Depicts students in nontraditional vocational areas. Includes interviews with male and female students who chose a nontraditional field of study and with program completers working in nontraditional careers. Lets students know that choosing a nontraditional career may be very rewarding intrinsically and monetarily. 3/4 in. Order from Illinois State Curriculum Center, Sangamon State University, Springfield, IL 62794.

NT13. *Choices/Changes: An Investigation of Alternative Occupational Role Models.* Mary Gilbert. Newton, MA: WEEA Publishing Center, 1982.
> Interviews numerous people pursuing nontraditional careers. The interviewees discuss what it is like to have nontraditional jobs, why they chose them, and how they have combined work and family. Order from 55 Chapel St., Suite 200, Newton, MA 02160.

NT14. *The Coal Employment Project: How Women Can Make Breakthroughs into Nontraditional Industries.* Washington, DC: U.S. Department of Labor, 1985.
> Describes a special initiative to improve opportunities for women who sought jobs in the predominately male coal mining industry, with the hope that similar efforts may be made in other industries where few women have been employed. Order from U.S. Department of Labor, Office of the Secretary, Women's Bureau, Washington, DC 20210.

NT15. "Conflict and the Female Principal." H. Lynn Erickson, *Phi Delta Kappan*, Dec. 1985, 289–91.
> Profiles a typical female school administrator and cites androgyny as a key to success.

NT16. *Corrections Presentation.* Brian S. Surprenant. Springfield, IL: Illinois State Board of Education, 1986.
> Discusses the benefits of women working in all-male correctional institutions. Part of the *Sex Equity in Law Enforcement*

and Corrections series (R). Order from Department of Adult, Vocational, and Technical Education, 100 N. First St., Springfield, IL 62777.

NT17. *Counseling Programs and Services for Women in Non-Traditional Occupations.* Helen S. Farmer. Columbus, OH: Ohio State University, 1978.

Examines opportunities, needs, and support systems relevant for women seeking to enter nontraditional professional or nonprofessional occupations. Order from ERIC Clearinghouse on Adult, Career, and Vocational Education, Center for Education and Training for Employment, 1900 Kenny Rd., Columbus, OH 43210.

NT18. *A Descriptive Study of Females Preparing for a Nontraditional Career in Aviation.* Charles L. Rodriguez. Master's thesis, Southern Illinois University at Carbondale, 1986.

Identifies the perceptions and factors that influenced women to enter a nontraditional program in aviation careers.

NT19. *Dreams of Flying.* Severo Perez. Videocassette. Sacramento, CA: State Department of Education, 1989.

Stresses the importance of education—finishing high school, enrolling in a community college or university, and selecting an occupational or academic major. Features Hispanic characters. Shows family and social barriers against nontraditional careers. Order from Illinois State Curriculum Center, Sangamon State University, Springfield, IL 62794.

NT20. *Eliminating Sexual Bias in Aviation Occupations.* Gary Eiff. Springfield, IL: Illinois State Board of Education, 1986.

Describes research into the stereotyping of females and the perceived sexual biases in aviation careers. Provides a workshop scope and format. Order from Department of Adult, Vocational, and Technical Education, 100 N. First St., Springfield, IL 62777.

NT21. *Equity in Corrections: A Generalized Planning Model.* T. Antoinette Ryan. Washington, DC: U.S. Department of Education, 1980.

Provides guidelines by which correctional agencies can develop plans that address the special needs, interests, and concerns of women and minorities entering or already employed in careers in corrections. Order from WEEA Publishing Center, 55 Chapel St., Suite 200, Newton, MA 02160.

NT22. *Equity Works*. 2 videocassettes. New York: Educational Equity Concepts, 1985.

Depicts highlights of a New York conference on excellence and equity. *Equity Works: 5 to 50+* includes speakers on equity in early childhood education, math, disability, athletics, and education for reentry women. *Equity Works: Vocational Education* features four nontraditional high school students and a vocational school principal. 20 min. each. An accompanying discussion guide provides short descriptions of the tapes and suggests ways to use them. Order from 114 E. 32nd St., New York, NY 10016.

NT23. *Exploring New Worlds: A Workbook on Trades and Technology for Women*. Margaret A. Nash. Madison, WI: University of Wisconsin, 1991.

Encourages girls and women to consider careers in higher paying occupations. Provides activities for use in classrooms or with individuals. Includes brief life stories of women successful in skilled trades and high-tech fields. Order from Center on Education and Work, University of Wisconsin-Madison, Department AM, l025 W. Johnson St., Madison, WI 53706.

NT24. *Factors Influencing Nontraditional Vocational Education Enrollments: A Literature Review*. Louise Vetter et al. Columbus, OH: National Center for Research in Vocational Education, 1979.

Reviews background information on the labor force and vocational education, factors influencing nontraditional enrollments, and strategies for increasing nontraditional enrollments. Order from Center on Education and Training for Employment, 1900 Kenny Rd., Columbus, OH 43210.

NT25. "Female Executives with Male Assistants (Don't Call Them Secretaries)." Sharon Johnson. *Working Woman*, Mar. 1985, 130–31.

Gives reasons why some female executives choose male assistants and why some men choose this career route.

NT26. *The Feminine Mystique.* Anne Grant. Videocassette. Newton, MA: WEEA Publishing Center, 1979.

Explores what it means to women to have more choices and opportunities in careers. Part of *Venture Beyond Stereotypes* program (GS). Order from 55 Chapel St., Suite 200, Newton, MA 02160.

NT27. "The Feminization of the Professional Work Force." *Business Week,* 17 Feb. 1986, 21.

Discusses trends that show women training for and entering into the ranks of professional fields in record numbers.

NT28. *From Here to There.* Mary Ellen Verheyden-Hilliard. Bethesda, MD: Equity Institute, 1983.

Presents a multimedia approach to exploring the apprentice-to-journeyworker career ladder with students in grades 1–9. Emphasizes that a journeyworker career (traditionally thought of as "men's work") is an option for girls as well as boys. Includes modules (lessons and filmstrips) and implementation for grades 1–2, 3–4, 5–6, 7–9 English/social studies, 7–9 math, and 7–9 physical education. Also includes guides for counselors, parents, and industry/labor leaders. Order from P.O. Box 30245, Bethesda, MD 20814.

NT29. *Futures Unlimited: Expanding Choices in Nontraditional Careers.* Arlene S. Chasek. New Brunswick, NJ: State University of New Jersey, 1985.

Describes a conference model meant for a wide range of female students in grades 7–12. Aims to make girls aware that most of them will be working most of their adult lives; to encourage students to take as much math, science, and industrial arts courses as possible in high school and to keep career options open; to expose students to careers they may not have considered; and to provide participants with exciting hands-on activities in math, science, computers, business, industrial arts, and technologies, in a supportive atmosphere designed especially for them. Order from Consortium for

Educational Equity, Rutgers, Kilmer Campus 4090, New Brunswick, NJ 08903.

NT30. *Futures Unlimited: Real People, Real Jobs.* 10 poster set. New Brunswick, NJ: State University of New Jersey, 1986.

Depicts 10 New Jersey female workers employed in nontraditional technical jobs with high-growth projects. Demonstrates a variety of exciting technological careers for which mathematics is a prerequisite. Order from Consortium for Educational Equity, Rutgers, Kilmer Campus 4090, State University of New Jersey, New Brunswick, NJ 08903.

NT31. *Go for It!* Videocassette. Juneau, AK: Alaska Department of Adult and Vocational Education, 1985.

Contains information designed for women (high school, postsecondary, or returning older students) who may have an interest in vocational education training, and discusses the types of occupations available in the trades. Demonstrates that women can successfully choose a career in construction-related trades. Provides a variety of successful role models, gives practical information on what high school courses and prerequisite skills are most useful, and explores the unique pressures and rewards for women choosing to work in the trades. Includes a discussion guide and posters. Order from Vocational Education Equity Program, Office of Adult and Vocational Education, Alaska Department of Education, Pouch F, Juneau, AL 99811.

NT32. *The Guidance Needs of Women.* Lenore W. Harmon. Information Series no. 149. Columbus, OH: National Center for Research in Vocational Education, 1979.

Focuses on barriers internal to women that prevent them from achieving occupational success in nontraditional jobs. Order from Center for Education and Training for Employment, 1900 Kenny Rd., Columbus, OH 43210.

NT33. "Helping Women Prepare for Principalships." Christa Metzger. *Phi Delta Kappan*, Dec. 1985, 292–96.

Describes an Arizona program that provides support to women educators who aspire to administrative positions.

NT34. *Historical Presentation.* Brian S. Surprenant. Slide presentation. Springfield, IL: Illinois State Board of Education, 1986.

> Discusses the historical development of the role of women in law enforcement and corrections. Part of the *Sex Equity in Law Enforcement and Corrections* series (R). 34 slides, 10 min. script. Order from Department of Adult, Vocational, and Technical Education, 100 N. First St., Springfield, IL 62777.

NT35. *Identification of Barriers and Strategies to Overcome the Barriers Pertaining to Nontraditional Job Opportunities for Women.* Denver, CO: State Board of Community Colleges, 1986.

> Contains a study of barriers for women entering nontraditional occupations and of strategies to overcome these barriers that was conducted in Colorado at the request of Wider Opportunities for Women (WOW). Order from Equity Unit of the State Board of Community Colleges and Occupational Education, 1313 Sherman St., Room 214, Denver CO 80203.

NT36. *Increasing Women's Access to Nontraditional Jobs.* Chicago, IL: Women Employed Institute, 1987.

> Considers occupational segregation, its effect on women, and Chicago's current record for promoting nontraditional careers for women. Gives recommendations for action. Order from 5 S. Wabash, Suite 415, Chicago, IL 60603.

NT37. *Interviewing for a Nontraditional Job.* Susan Jones Sears. Columbus, OH: Ohio State University, 1984.

> Enhances job-seeking and interviewing skills for women seeking nontraditional positions. Includes sections on misconceptions one may encounter, on preparing a resume and interviewing, and on discrimination in the workplace. Order from Center for Sex Equity in Vocational Education, 123 Townshend Hall, 1885 Neil Ave., Columbus, OH 43210.

NT38. *It's Her Future.* Marilyn Levin. Videocassette. Newton, MA: WEEA Publishing Center, 1979.

> Encourages young women to explore the range of training opportunities and benefits available in nontraditional ca-

reers. Includes a discussion guide that shows ways in which parents and educators can help young women take advantage of nontraditional opportunities and benefits. 3/4 in., 17 min. The video information is also available in booklet form. Order from 55 Chapel St., Suite 200, Newton, MA 02160.

NT39. *It's Your Right.* Joyce Kaser. Andover, MA: Network, 1984.

Provides a handbook for secondary students considering a nontraditional field of study. Order from Mid-Atlantic Center for Sex Equity, 290 S. Main St., Andover, MA 01810.

NT40. *Job Options for Women in the 80's.* Washington, DC: U.S. Department of Labor, 1980.

Provides guidance to women making decisions about their lives and work. Helps them take advantage of the opportunities open to them. Order from Women's Bureau, Washington, DC 20210.

NT41. *Just Between Sisters: Futures Unlimited.* Videocassette. New Brunswick, NJ: State University of New Jersey, 1986.

Profiles several minority women who have chosen nontraditional technical career paths. VHS, 30 min. Order from Consortium for Education Equity, Rutgers, Kilmer Campus 4090, New Brunswick, NJ 08903.

NT42. *Keep Your Options Open: Rhode Island Women in Technical Fields Tell Their Own Stories.* Joan Mascovitch Webb. Providence, RI: Rhode Island College, 1987.

Includes short biographical sketches by women in technical professions in Rhode Island.

NT43. *Looking for More Than a Few Good Women in Traditionally Male Fields.* Julie Kuhn Ehrhart and Bernice R. Sandler. Washington, DC: Association of American Colleges, 1987.

Discusses why more women are not studying and completing degrees in traditionally male fields and what postsecondary institutions can do to help remedy this situation. Focuses on women students' experiences in traditionally male programs at the college and university level. Order from 1818 R St., NW, Washington, DC 20009.

NT44. *Meeting the Challenge: Women in Aviation.* Videocassette. Springfield, IL: Illinois State Board of Education, 1986.
> Interviews challenged, enthused, and successful women currently working in aviation-related fields. 18 min. Order from Illinois State Curriculum Center, Sangamon State University, Springfield, IL 62794.

NT45. *Minorities in Engineering.* Booklet. Chicago, IL: Illinois Bell, n.d.
> Describes ways minorities can impact the field of engineering.

NT46. *Missouri Vocational Opportunities Program.* Jefferson City, MO: Missouri Department of Elementary and Secondary Education, 1987.
> Contains a resource guide for nontraditional careers. Order from Division of Vocational and Adult Education, P.O. Box 480, Jefferson City, MO 65102.

NT47. *Mythbusters.* Patricia Mitchell. Videocassette. Jersey City, NJ: Jersey City State College, 1987.
> Encourages young women to consider traditionally male trades. Emphasizes the personal satisfaction and financial benefits of entering such trades as carpentry and welding, and presents the obstacles females might encounter and ways to cope with them. Features minority females. Order from Illinois State Curriculum Center, Sangamon State University, Springfield, IL 62794.

NT48. *New Choices: Women in Non-Traditional Careers.* Kimberly Otis. Videocassette. New York: New York City Board of Education, 1990.
> Profiles women in nontraditional careers, who tell about how they got into the job, the pay they receive, the discrimination against them (if any) and the advantages they now have that they did not have before. Uses lively music and a student dance group to keep the interest level up. Order from Illinois State Curriculum Center, Sangamon State University, Springfield, IL 62794.

NT49. *New Facts about Management Women.* New York: Catalyst, 1985.

Gives recent statistics that illustrate the progress women are making in breaking into management ranks. Order from 250 Park Ave. South, New York, NY 10003.

NT50. *New Steps on the Career Ladder.* Audrey Denecke. 2 vols. Springfield, IL: Illinois State Board of Education, 1981.

Includes a curriculum guide, pɪ ɔgram model, and resource guide that provides educators witɪɪ the curriculum materials, systems information, programs, and resources needed for women to pursue nontraditional and apprenticeable occupations. The curriculum is designed for young women planning their careers and constitutes a complete eight-week course that traces the history of women workers, explains the apprenticeship process, suggests nontraditional professional employment options, outlines strategies for self-assessment, and reviews equal employment legislation. Order from Department of Adult, Vocational, and Technical Education, 100 N. First St., Springfield, IL 62777.

NT51. "The New Strong Women in TV—and How They're Changing the Industry." Karen Stabiner. *New Woman*, Oct. 1986, 115–20.

Discusses the emergence in television of more women than in the past. Considers the people behind the cameras and scripts.

NT52. *The Nuts and Bolts of NTO.* Jo Schuchat. Metuchen, NJ: Scarecrow, 1986.

Updates *The Nuts and Bolts of NTO: A Handbook for Recruitment, Training, Support Services, and Placement of Women in Nontraditional Occupations* (NT). Contains an in-depth discussion of recruitment, training, and placement of adult women in nontraditional occupations, particularly skilled or vocational/technical occupations.

NT53. *The Nuts and Bolts of NTO: A Handbook for Recruitment, Training, Support Services, and Placement of Women in Nontraditional Occupations.* Jo Schuchat. New York: Women's Action Alliance, 1981.

Discusses recruitment, training, and placement of adult women in occupations that are nontraditional, particularly skilled or vocational/technical occupations. Companion to *Time for a Change: A Woman's Guide to Nontraditional Occupations* (NT). Order from 370 Lexington Ave., New York, NY 10017.

NT54. *Placing Rural Minority Women in Training Situations for Nontraditional Jobs.* Alice Paris. Epes, AL: Federation of Southern Cooperatives, 1979.

Increases the low-income, rural, minority women's potential in the labor market by linking them with nontraditional job opportunities and training programs. Details entire process, from staff selection to evaluation. Includes a list of agencies and resources and outlines valuable strategies. Order from WEEA Publishing Center, 55 Chapel St., Suite 200, Newton, MA 02160.

NT55. *Putting It All Together: A Model Program for Women Entering Engineering.* William K. LeBold. Newton, MA: WEEA Publishing Center, 1982.

Contains a model program that gives first-year college women the opportunity to explore a wide range of engineering careers. Shows how to establish a program that includes lectures by women scientists, supportive counseling sessions, and unpressured labs. Includes a slide and tape presentation entitled *Engineering Skills and Career Planning: A Model Program.* Order from 55 Chapel St., Suite 200, Newton, MA 02160.

NT56. *Real People, Real Jobs.* New Brunswick, NJ: State University of New Jersey, 1982.

Provides guides to elementary and secondary teachers for increasing student awareness of the expanding range of job options. Includes pictures of posters (not available) depicting nontraditional workers, and gives a job description, educational requirements, wages, occupational outlook, related jobs, and tools of the trade for each occupation. Includes several student activities. Order from Consortium for Educational Equity, Rutgers, Kilmer Campus 4090, New Brunswick, NJ 08903.

NT57. *The Report Card 4: Women in Educational Administration.* Myra Sadker. Washington, DC: Mid-Atlantic Center for Sex Equity, 1984.

Summarizes research on women in educational administration. Order from 5010 Wisconsin Ave., NW, Suite 310, Washington, DC 20016.

NT58. *Resource Guide for Sex Equity in Law Enforcement/ Corrections.* Brian S. Surprenant. Springfield, IL: Illinois State Board of Education, 1986.

Provides abstracts of articles, publications, and books that discuss gender equity in law enforcement and corrections. Part of the *Sex Equity in Law Enforcement and Corrections* series (R). Order from Illinois State Curriculum Center, Sangamon State University, Springfield, IL 62794.

NT59. *Sex-Fair Artwork.* Columbus, OH: Ohio State University, 1986.

Contains reproducible sex-fair artwork that portrays females and males in nontraditional roles and activities. Order from Center for Sex Equity in Vocational Education, 123 Townshend Hall, 1885 Neil Ave., Columbus, OH 43215.

NT60. "Sex-Role Identity and Work Perceptions of Nontraditional Vocational Graduates." Penny L. Burge. *Journal of Vocational Education Research*, 8.2 (Spring 1983): 41–54.

Addresses the following research questions: What are the attitudes held by nontraditional workers toward their work? What attracted nontraditional workers to their field of employment? How do nontraditional workers evaluate their performance on the job? What are the gender role identities of nontraditional workers? What are the relationships among the study's major variables and the demographic information of the sample?

NT61. "She Gets High Marks as Trustee in Village." Pete Rosenbery. *Southern Illinoisan*, 14 Mar. 1986.

Introduces Marci Garrett, a 22-year-old resident of Energy, Illinois, who was appointed to serve on the Village Board of Trustees.

NT62. "She's the Boss." Larry Davis. *Southern Illinoisan*, 2 Feb. 1986.

> Introduces Anne Gaylord, a project manager for a construction company.

NT63. *Sports Need You: A Working Model for the Equity Professional.* Susan P. Schafer. Denver, CO: Colorado Department of Education, 1984.

> Tells how to increase the number of women and minorities in athletic coaching, officiating, administration, and governance. Order from Title IX/Sex Equity Program, Colorado Department of Education, Denver, CO 80201.

NT64. *Stepping Out.* Christy Bertelson, Liz Carlson, and Jeffrey Ham. Filmstrip series. Madison, WI: Wisconsin Vocational Studies Center, n.d.

> Helps women decide whether to enter a nontraditional occupation. Includes facilitator's guidebook and participants' handout. Order from 964 Educational Sciences Building, 1025 W. Johnson St., Madison, WI 53706.

NT65. *Succeeding in a Job.* Susan Jones Sears. Columbus, OH: Ohio State University, 1984.

> Contains a student workbook on job-keeping skills for women in nontraditional positions. Includes sections on responsible work attitudes and habits, handling sexual harassment, and communicating effectively. Companion to *Interviewing for a Nontraditional Job* (NT). Order from Center for Sex Equity in Vocational Education, 123 Townshend Hall, 1885 Neil Ave., Columbus, OH 43215.

NT66. *Take It from Us . . . You Can Be an Engineer.* Fairfield, CT: General Electric Company, 1986.

> Includes testimonials of young engineers who describe their jobs and tells students how to prepare for a career in engineering. Includes nontraditional role models. Order from General Electric Company, Educational Communications Program, Fairfield, CT 06431.

NT67. *They're Trying Something Different and Liking It!* Brochure. Springfield, IL: Illinois State Board of Education, 1980.

Provides a collection of success stories about students in nontraditional vocational education programs in Illinois. Order from Department of Adult, Vocational, and Technical Education, 100 N. First St., Springfield, IL 62777.

NT68. *The Third Sex.* Patricia A. McBroom. New York: William Morrow and Company, 1986.

Profiles the personality and life-style of the new professional woman. Based on the testimony of 44 professional women working in finance in New York and San Francisco.

NT69. *Time for a Change: A Woman's Guide to Nontraditional Occupations.* Constance Drake Cauley. New York: Women's Action Alliance, 1981.

Provides a guide for women of all ages and backgrounds who are working outside the home or thinking about it and who think a nontraditional career may suit them. Includes information on myths regarding women in nontraditional careers and on barriers to entry, specific information on various careers, and methods for proceeding. Companion to *The Nuts and Bolts of NTO: A Handbook for Recruitment, Training, Support Services, and Placement of Women in Nontraditional Occupations* (NT). Order from 370 Lexington Ave., New York, NY 10017.

NT70. "Top Women Executives Find Path to Power Is Strewn with Hurdles." Helen Rogan. *Wall Street Journal*, 25 Oct. 1984, 35.

Highlights common obstacles that female executives need to overcome for success.

NT71. *Training the Woman to Know Her Place.* Sandra L. Bem and Daryl J. Bem. Stanford, CA: Stanford University, 1975.

Considers the social antecedents of women in the world of work. Order from Department of Psychology, Stanford University, Stanford, CA 94305.

NT72. *Vocational Education Programs Offer Differences That Count in Your Future.* Brochure. Lafayette, LA: Louisiana State Department of Education, n.d.

Promotes nontraditional vocational study. Order from Charles Bonvillain, Lafayette Parish School Board, P.O. Drawer 2158, Lafayette, LA 70502.

NT73. "We Need All the Support We Can Get." Maria Dolan. *VocEd*, Apr. 1980, 28–30.

Contains the testimony of a 25-year-old female diesel mechanic. Discusses the obvious and subtle obstacles to entry and success in a nontraditional occupation and requests that vocational education address these issues.

NT74. *What's It Like to Be a Technician.* Fairfield, CT: General Electric Company, 1983.

Describes opportunities open to young men and women who wish to be technicians and gives information on preparing for this type of career. Includes sex-fair photographs. Order from General Electric Company, Educational Communications Program, Fairfield, CT 06431.

NT75. *What's It Like to Be an Engineer.* Fairfield, CT: General Electric Company, 1983.

Describes the work engineers do and gives information on preparing for a career in engineering. Includes sex-fair photographs. Order from General Electric Company, Educational Communications Program, Fairfield, CT 06431.

NT76. *Why Not Me? Women in Non-Traditional Jobs.* New York: National Child Labor Committee, 1984.

Contains a module designed for small businesses that employ young people. Develops strategies for dealing with worker's attitudes toward women in nontraditional jobs, reducing adjustment problems, building productive team workers, and solving problems of sex discrimination.

NT77. "Wife, Mother, and State University President." MacDonald Meade. *Review Weekly* (Maplewood MN), 1986.

Discusses the achievements and family life of Dr. Reatha Clark King, president of Metropolitan State University in Maplewood, Minnesota.

NT78. "Women Administrators: Profiles of Success." Lillian C. Woo. *Phi Delta Kappan*, Dec. 1985, 285–88.

Describes the traits that characterize women who have made
it to the upper echelons of educational administration.

NT79. *Women and the Military.* Washington, DC: Women's
Equity Action League, 1983.

Provides an overview of the military and of the individual
services, an analysis of timely issues, and a bibliography.
Includes fact sheets on recruitment statistics and policies,
single parents, women and the combat exclusion laws, the
Former Spouse Protection Act, and sexual harassment. Order from 1250 I St., NW, Suite 305, Washington, DC
20005.

NT80. *Women and Their Preparation for Professional and Mana-
gerial Careers.* Rosalind K. Loring. Information Series no. 168.
Columbus, OH: National Center for Research in Vocational
Education, 1979.

Examines issues in counseling, educational programs, and
support systems. Order from Center for Education and
Training for Employment, 1900 Kenny Rd., Columbus,
OH 43210.

NT81. *Women and Wilderness.* Anne LaBastille. Santa Rosa,
CA: National Women's History Project, 1980.

Considers the historical role of women in America's frontier
wilderness and contrasts that role with the ever-changing
involvement of women in the outdoors today. Order from
P.O. Box 3716, Santa Rosa, CA 95402.

NT82. "Women Engineers." Jean Ness. *Alumnus* (magazine
of the Southern Illinois University Alumni Association), Fall
1984, 6–7.

Provides information about the focus on women in engineering at Southern Illinois University at Carbondale. Includes career information and discusses the importance of
math and science to a career in engineering.

NT83. *Women in Apprenticeship . . . There's a Future in It!*
Leaflet no. 58. Washington, DC: U.S. Department of Labor,
1980.

Provides an overview of the opportunities for women in
apprenticeship training. Order from U.S. Department of

Labor, Office of the Secretary, Women's Bureau, Washington, DC 20210.

NT84. *Women in Engineering Survey.* Chris S. Anderson. Houghton, MI: Michigan Technological University, 1985.

Contains results and conclusions of a follow-up study done with the participants of the Women in Engineering program from 1979 to 1984. Order from Department of Engineering, Michigan Technological University, Houghton, MI 49931.

NT85. *Women in Finance.* Diane C. Smith. Lincolnwood, IL: VGM Career Horizons, 1981.

Interviews 12 women in finance careers.

NT86. *Women in Higher Wage Occupations Resource Manual.* Margaret Tulley. Madison, WI: University of Wisconsin, 1991.

Contains classroom activities and worksheets to help students understand the economic impact their career choice will have on their lives. Includes information on women in the work force, occupational segregation, and nontraditional careers. Order from Center on Education and Work, University of Wisconsin-Madison, Department AM, 1025 W. Johnson St., Madison, WI 53706.

NT87. *Women in Law Enforcement.* Peter Horne. Springfield, IL: Charles C. Thomas, 1980.

Examines the historical and current role of policewomen in policing and recommends future changes to increase equality in law enforcement.

NT88. *Women in Nontraditional Careers (WINC) Curriculum Guide.* Rosalind Hamar, Andrea Hunter, and Madeline Moore. Portland, OR: Northwest Regional Educational Laboratory, 1981.

Serves as a teaching tool for educators, counselors, youth workers, and others who wish to help young and adult women explore the issues related to women, work, and nontraditional employment. Includes a nine-unit course that can be taught in a semester, over a full school year, or as a supplement to other in-school curricula or out-of-school employability programs. The units are "Women and Work—

History," "Women and Work—Today and Tomorrow," "Community-Based Job Exploration," "Sex Role Stereotyping," "Access to Careers," "Career Success Styles," "Job Hunting for Nontraditional Jobs," "Nontraditional Life/Job Survival Skills," and "Career and Life Planning." Each unit includes activities and activity resources. Order from 300 S.W. Sixth Ave., Portland, OR 97204.

NT89. *Women in Nontraditional Careers (WINC) Journal.* Portland, OR: Northwest Regional Educational Laboratory, 1981.

Integrates fact, humor, and instruction with blank journal pages, to stimulate and guide young women to explore and write down their feelings about their career planning. May be used in conjunction with *Women in Nontraditional Careers Curriculum Guide* (NT). Order from 300 S.W. Sixth Ave., Portland, OR 97204.

NT90. *Women in Technologies: A Support System for Entering Nontraditional Occupations.* Anita Jaehn. Rochester, NY: Monroe Community College, 1983.

Reports on a project designed to recruit women for the Engineering Technologies degree programs at Monroe Community College, to help them prepare for entrance into these degree programs, and to provide support for them once they are enrolled. Order from 1000 E. Henrietta Rd., Rochester, NY 14623.

NT91. *Women in Technology.* Elizabeth M. Broman. Lincoln, NE: Policy Research Office, 1984.

Discusses why women are now underrepresented in technological jobs. Includes recommendations for improvement. Order from Room 1321, State Capitol, Box 94601, Lincoln, NE 68509.

NT92. "Women in Technology." *Technology Review*, Nov./Dec. 1984, 29–52.

Contains the articles "Women in Science and Engineering: Why So Few?" "Women Working: A Field Report," "High-Energy Physics: A Male Preserve," and "Will Women Engineers Make A Difference?"

NT93. "Women in the Military." Eloise Engle. *National Forum*, Fall 1981, 26.

> Discusses the advances women have made in military careers.

NT94. *Women Who Work with Animals.* Bill Gutman. Santa Rosa, CA: National Women's History Project, 1982.

> Contains the stories of six women who have devoted their lives to working with animals in various ways. Each woman has had to work hard to be successful, and some have had to prove that women can do jobs that were once held only by men. Order from P.O. Box 3716, Santa Rosa, CA 95402.

NT95. *Women's Work: Physical Preparation.* Christine Shelton Walters. Manchester, NY: New Hampshire Vocational Technical College, 1978.

> Provides guidance for developing a fitness program that physically prepares female students for the demands of some technical nontraditional careers. Order from Project FATE, New Hampshire Vocational Technical College, Manchester, NH 03031.

NT96. *Working Equal.* Videocassette. Columbus, OH: Ohio State University, 1980.

> Helps students broaden their views of occupational choices and encourages them to consider enrollment in nontraditional vocational education courses. Order from Center for Education and Training for Employment, 1900 Kenny Rd., Columbus, OH 43210.

NT97. *A World for Women in Engineering.* Booklet. Chicago, IL: Illinois Bell, n.d.

> Considers how women can impact the traditionally male-dominated field of engineering. Order from 225 W. Randolph, Chicago, IL 61611.

NT98. *You Can Do It in Technical Careers.* Linda Grace. 9 videocassette series. Springfield, IL: Illinois State Board of Education, 1988.

> Encourages men and women to pursue whatever type of career they desire, even though it may be nontraditional. Focuses on following your dreams and choosing what you

would like to do for a lifetime career. Pictures men and women in nontraditional fields. Series includes automotive technology, construction technology, dental hygiene, electronics technology, law enforcement, office specialties, physical therapy, and tool and manufacturing. Order from Illinois State Curriculum Center, Sangamon State University, Springfield, IL 62794.

18 Pregnant and Parenting Teens (PT)

PT1. *Adolescent Pregnancy and Parenting: Evaluating School Policies and Programs from a Sex Equity Perspective.* Margaret C. Dunkle. Washington, DC: Council of Chief State School Officers, 1985.

> Helps schools eliminate policies and practices that discriminate against pregnant and parenting teens in violation of Title IX. Increases awareness of issues. Order from Resource Center on Educational Equity, Suite 379, 400 N. Capitol St., NW, Washington, DC 20001.

PT2. *Adolescent Pregnancy and Parenting: School Focused Strategies for State Policymakers.* Washington, DC: Council of Chief State School Officers, 1985.

> Discusses how educators can provide leadership in addressing the problems facing pregnant and parenting teens. Order from Resource Center on Educational Equity, Suite 379, 400 N. Capitol St., NW, Washington, DC 20001.

PT3. *Adolescent Pregnancy and Parenting Project: Directory of State Officials.* Washington, DC: National Association of State Boards of Education, 1985.

> Lists persons who may be contacted to obtain state-by-state information on adolescent pregnancy and parenting policies. Order from Resource Center on Educational Equity, Suite 379, 400 N. Capitol St., NW, Washington, DC 20001.

PT4. *Becoming and Being a Teen Parent: A Literature Review.* Helen L. Carlson. Duluth, MN: University of Duluth, 1985.

> Reviews almost 300 sources of information on teen parenting and makes specific recommendations for programs for teen parents.

PT5. *Breaking Out: Career Choices for Teenage Parents.* A. Frances Lindner. Videocassette. Madison, WI: University of Wisconsin, 1988.

> Shows former teen parents in nontraditional, higher wage occupations, teens currently parents and in school, and

women in nontraditional jobs. 18 min. Order from Center on Education and Work, University of Wisconsin-Madison, Department AM, 1025 W. Johnson St., Madison, WI 53706.

PT6. *Building Self-Sufficiency: A Guide to Vocational and Employment Services for Teenage Parents.* Denise F. Polit. Jefferson City, MO: Humanalysis, 1986.

Provides a handbook aimed at teen parent program staff, youth employment program staff, teen parent advocates, vocational educators, sex equity coordinators, private industry councils, policymakers, and all people working to enhance the life options of young mothers and fathers. Order from P.O. Box 1123, Jefferson City, MO 65102.

PT7. *Career Orientation and Preparation for Teen Parents Curriculum.* Vicki Whipple. Curriculum guide. Springfield, IL: Illinois State Board of Education, 1987.

Provides career orientation and preparation for teen parents, focusing on nontraditional occupations and current labor market trends.

PT8. "Children Having Children." Claudia Wallis. *Time,* 9 Dec. 1985.

Discusses teen pregnancy and teen parenting.

PT9. *A Community of Caring.* Eunice Kennedy Shriver. New York: Walker Publishing Company, 1982.

Contains 21 teaching modules structured to help adolescent parents understand pregnancy, birth, and child care. Also addresses such practical decisions as employment, marriage, and adoption.

PT10. *Competency-Based Instructional Units for Teenage Parenting.* Flora C. Armstrong. Curriculum guide. VA: Virginia Department of Education, 1983.

Includes units on nutrition and personal care, child care and development, personal development and parenthood, money management, and community resources.

PT11. *Do I Have a Daddy? A Story about a Single-Parent Child.* Jeanne Warren Lindsay. Buena Park, CA: Morning Glory, 1982.

Explains how a single mother tells her son that his father left after he was born. Includes suggestions for answering the child's questions. Order from 6595M San Haraldo Way, Buena Park, CA 90620.

PT12. *Educating Pregnant and Parenting Teens: Our Responsibility, Our Challenge.* Jeanne Warren Lindsay. Buena Park, CA: Morning Glory, 1985.

Discusses teen pregnancy and gives suggestions on how school districts can assist and encourage young mothers. Order from 6595M San Haraldo Way, Buena Park, CA 90620.

PT13. *Female Dropouts: A New Perspective.* Janice Early, Virginia Roach, and Katherine Fraser. Alexandria, VA: National Association of State Boards of Education, 1987.

Considers research focused on dropping out, female socialization, cognitive styles, and teacher interactions, to shed light on the factors relating to a young woman's decision to drop out of school. Order from 701 N. Fairfax St., Suite 340, Alexandria, VA 22314.

PT14. *Good Beginnings: Parenting for Young Parents.* Judith L. Evans. 8 booklets. New York: Manpower Demonstration Research Corporation, 1985.

Provides information developed for use by the adolescent parent, beginning with pregnancy and continuing through the child's third year. Focuses on the young parent, her development, and infant/toddler development. Order from 3 Park Ave., New York, NY 10016.

PT15. *Here's Help: Independent Study Curriculum Guide for Pregnant and Parenting Teens.* Jeanne Warren Lindsay. Buena Park, CA: Morning Glory, 1986.

Details independent study assignments to be used with *Teenage Pregnancy: A New Beginning* and *Teens Parenting: The Challenge of Babies and Toddlers* (PT). Order from 6595M San Haraldo Way, Buena Park, CA 90620.

PT16. *Peer Education Programs.* Ling Chin and Marjorie B. Dahlin. Washington, DC: Center for Population Options, 1983.

Describes several successful peer education programs for sexuality education and gives guidelines for setting up a new program. Order from 2031 Florida Ave., NW, Washington, DC 20009.

PT17. *Pregnant Too Soon: Adoption Is an Option.* Jeanne Warren Lindsay. St. Paul, MN: EMC Publishing, 1980.

Focuses on the decision of a young parent choosing whether to raise his or her child or to relinquish the child for adoption. Order from 300 York Ave., St. Paul, MN 55101.

PT18. *The Report Card 5: Education and the Teenage Pregnancy Puzzle.* Jill E. Reid and Margaret C. Dunkle. Washington, DC: Network, 1985.

Discusses the causes of teen pregnancy, who is at risk, the costs, what schools and educators can do, and what some schools are doing. Order from Mid-Atlantic Center for Sex Equity, 5010 Wisconsin Ave., NW, Suite 310, Washington, DC 20016.

PT19. *Small Group Workshop.* Sarah Renner. Washington, DC: Center for Population Options, 1983.

Describes several small group workshop program models for sexuality education and gives guidelines for setting up a new program. Includes a resource listing. Order from 2031 Florida Ave., NW, Washington, DC 20009.

PT20. *Speaking for Ourselves.* Videocassette. Springfield, IL: Illinois State Board of Education, 1987.

Presents a frank discussion by teen parents of the problems they have faced. Order from Illinois State Curriculum Center, Sangamon State University, Springfield, IL 62794.

PT21. *Starting Out . . . A Job-Finding Handbook for Teen Parents.* Neva N. Harden. Santa Fe, NM: State Department of Education, 1986.

Provides a practical guide to finding a job (not a lifetime career) and includes such issues as work permits, social security, budgeting, choosing a first home, and day care. Order from Vocational-Technical and Adult Education, State Department of Education, Santa Fe, NM 87501.

PT22. *The Teen Parents Collaboration: Strengthening Services to Teen Mothers.* James A. Riccio. New York: Manpower Demonstration Research, 1985.

Contains an evaluation of Project Redirection, a program for low-income, pregnant, and parenting teen. Order from 3 Park Ave., New York, NY 10016.

PT23. *Teenage Parents: Making It Work.* A. Frances Lindner and Leanne Law. Videocassette. Madison, WI: University of Wisconsin, 1988.

Follows a teen mother through a day, raising issues concerning various needs, and provides the solutions teen mothers have found successful. 17 min. Order from Center on Education and Work, University of Wisconsin-Madison, Department AM, 1025 W. Johnson St., Madison, WI 53706.

PT24. *Teenage Pregnancy: A New Beginning.* Linda Barr. Curriculum guide. Albuquerque, NM: New Futures, 1978.

Discusses changes in the female body, how the baby develops, how to take care of yourself during pregnancy, and making decisions about school, family, marriage, and the future.

PT25. *Teenage Single Parent Initiative: Education for Employment.* Concept paper. Chicago, IL: Illinois Caucus on Teenage Pregnancy, 1985.

Reflects the collaborative efforts of the Illinois Caucus on Teenage Pregnancy, the Ounce of Prevention Fund, and Parents Too Soon to develop an integrated system that would enhance single teen parents' employability. Includes program overview, objectives, organization, and task plans.

PT26. *Teens Parenting: The Challenge of Babies and Toddlers.* Jeanne Warren Lindsay. Buena Park, CA: Morning Glory, 1981.

Records teen parents' discussions of infant and child development, childproofing, fathers' involvement, cost of child rearing, community resource help, discipline, single parenting, three-generation living, and the need for education and job training for mothers. Order from 6595M San Haraldo Way, Buena Park, CA 90620.

PT27. *The Three Generation Family*. Elizabeth Wampler. Indianapolis, IN: Consumer and Homemaking Community Project, 1984.

> Addresses the problems and conflict areas between family members when teen parents move back home to raise their young. Order from State Board of Vocational and Technical Education, 100 N. Senate Ave., Indianapolis, IN 46204.

PT28. *A Time for Transition*. New York: National Child Labor Committee, 1985.

> Reports on a study that examined teen pregnancy and our social institutions' inability to prepare teen parents to support themselves. Includes a resource listing. Order from 1501 Broadway, Room 111, New York, NY 10036.

PT29. *Training for Transition*. Elizabeth McGee. New York: Manpower Demonstration Research Corporation, 1985.

> Contains employability curriculum for teen mothers. Order from 3 Park Ave., New York, NY 10016.

PT30. *Working with Childbearing Adolescents*. Linda Barr. Albuquerque, NM: New Futures, 1986.

> Provides a guide for use with *Teenage Pregnancy: A New Beginning* (PT). Includes sections on adolescent parents' needs and services, adolescent development and teen sexuality, teens as parents, and working with pregnant teens.

19 Recruitment (R)

R1. *Corrections Recruitment Presentation.* Brian S. Surprenant. Springfield, IL: Illinois State Board of Education, 1986.
Illustrates duties of correctional officers in five correctional facilities located in Southern Illinois, with an emphasis on female officers. Part of the *Sex Equity in Law Enforcement and Corrections* series (R). Order from Department of Adult, Vocational, and Technical Education, 100 N. First St., Springfield, IL 62777.

R2. *Expand-A-Pac.* James Mahrt. Wayne, MI: NETWORK Project, 1983.
Presents many effective strategies for encouraging nontraditional enrollments in vocational programs. Describes each strategy, explains its usefulness, tells how to implement it and who should be responsible for implementation, identifies each target group, and estimates the cost of implementing each strategy. Order from Wayne County Intermediate School District, 33500 Van Born Rd., Wayne, MI 48184.

R3. *Fair Recruitment: The Model and Strategies.* Beverly Stitt and Marcia Anderson. Springfield, IL: Illinois State Board of Education, 1980.
Provides 50 specific recruitment strategies designed to be fair regarding gender, race, culture, age, and handicap. Discusses student recruitment on three levels: into vocational education, into specific vocational institutions, and into specific vocational education programs. Order from Curriculum Publications Clearinghouse, 47 Horriban Hall, Western Illinois University, Macomb, IL 61455.

R4. "Hidden Inequities Can Be Overcome." Janice R. Mokros. *VocEd*, May 1984, 39–41.
Discusses hidden ways in which the qualifications for entry into vocational programs may disproportionately bar certain groups from entry, even when there is no intent to do so.

R5.   *How to Encourage Girls to Select and Remain in Nontraditional Courses.* Charlotte H. Clarke. New Brunswick, NJ: State University of New Jersey, 1982.

> Gives guidance counselors strategies for the recruitment and retention of female students in courses that are nontraditional (may be adapted for male students). Order from Consortium for Educational Equity, Rutgers, Kilmer Campus 4090, New Brunswick, NJ 08903.

R6.   *Law Enforcement Recruitment Presentation.* Brian S. Surprenant. Slide presentation. Springfield, IL: Illinois State Board of Education, 1986.

> Interviews two male police chiefs, one female police chief, one male deputy police chief, and one female police officer concerning the attitudes and abilities of women in law enforcement. Part of the *Sex Equity in Law Enforcement and Corrections* series (R). 40 slides, 18 min. script. Order from Department of Adult, Vocational, and Technical Education, 100 N. First St., Springfield, IL 62777.

R7.   *Model for Recruitment, Retention, and Placement of Female Students in Vocational Education Programs Which Have Traditionally Been for Males.* James A. Knight. Columbus, OH: Ohio Department of Education, 1980.

> Describes a model based on research visits to schools particularly successful in recruiting, retaining, and placing female students in traditionally male vocational programs. Includes a section on holding a sex equity workshop for school personnel. Order from Division of Vocational Education, 65 S. Front St., Columbus, OH 43215.

R8.   *Sex Equity in Law Enforcement and Corrections.* Brian S. Surprenant. Slide presentation series. Springfield, IL: Illinois State Board of Education, 1986.

> Includes a resource guide and five slide modules: "Corrections Presentation," "Corrections Recruitment Presentation," "Historical Presentation," "Law Enforcement Presentation," "Law Enforcement Recruitment Presentation," and "Resource Guide for Sex Equity in Law Enforcement/Cor-

rection." Order from Department of Adult, Vocational, and Technical Education, 100 N. First St., Springfield, IL 62777.

R9. *Sex Equity Is Being Able to Do Your Own Thing.* Poster. Springfield, IL: Illinois State Board of Education, 1986.
Depicts nontraditional vocational students in work settings. Order from Department of Adult, Vocational, and Technical Education, 100 N. First St., Springfield, IL 62777.

R10. *Spotlight: Creative Initiatives That Work.* Pamphlet. New York, NY: Catalyst, 1987.
Contains brief sketches of four successful initiatives for recruiting, retaining, and developing qualified women employees. Order from 250 Park Ave. South, New York, NY 10003.

R11. *Strategies for Recruiting Women in Nontraditional Careers.* Beverly Stitt and Tom Stitt. Springfield, IL: Illinois Department of Commerce and Community Affairs, 1990.
Includes 20 complete recruitment strategies designed to interest women in pursuing a nontraditional career.

R12. *Strategies for Recruitment and Retention of Minority Staff in Michigan Vocational Education Programs* and *Strategies for Recruitment and Retention of Minority Students in Michigan Vocational Education Programs.* Companion pieces. Detroit, MI: CRW Associates, 1985.
Provides specific activities that result in increased minority hiring and outlines strategies for increasing student numbers. Order from 685 Pallister Ave., Detroit, MI 48202.

20

Special Needs (SN)

SN1. *Achieving Equity in Education Programs for Disabled Women and Girls.* Washington, DC: Council of Chief State School Officers, 1986.

> Increases educators' awareness of sex equity concerns and identifies particular ways in which sex bias and gender role stereotyping limit the educational and occupational opportunities of disabled students. Workshop manual format. Order from Resource Center on Educational Equity, 400 N. Capitol St., NW, Suite 379, Washington, DC 20001.

SN2. *Barrier Free.* Linda Marks and Harilyn Rousso. New York: YWCA, 1991.

> Examines important issues that disabled young women—like all young women—face: career exploration, independent living, and sexuality. Order from WEEA Publishing Center, 55 Chapel St., Suite 200, Newton, MA 02160.

SN3. *Disabled and Female: Double Jeopardy.* Ann Yrcisin. Menomonie, WI: University of Wisconsin-Stout, n.d.

> Discusses the double jeopardy of being disabled and female in selecting a career. Order from Services for Students with Disabilities Director, University of Wisconsin-Stout, Menomonie, WI 54751.

SN4. *Don't Go to Your Room . . . and Other Affirmations of Empowerment for Women with Disabilities.* Videocassette. Portland, OR: Access Oregon, 1990.

> Addresses the double barrier of being a woman and having a disability. Over a dozen women talk openly about issues they face in employment, relationships, sexuality, abuse, health, parenting, and empowering themselves. 60 min. Order from WEEA Publishing Center, 55 Chapel St., Suite 200, Newton, MA 02160.

SN5. *Equity for the Disadvantaged from a School Board Member's Perspective.* Carol Schwartz. R and D Series no. 214N. Columbus, OH: National Center for Research in Vocational Education, 1982.

Describes equity in vocational education from the perspective of the educationally or economically disadvantaged person. Highlights the present conditions of the disadvantaged and recommends improvements in vocational education. Order from Center on Education and Training for Employment, 1900 Kenny Rd., Columbus, OH 43210.

SN6. *Equity from a Bilingual Education Perspective.* Jo Ann Crandall. R and D Series no. 214D. Columbus, OH: National Center for Research in Vocational Education, 1982.

Describes the special needs of adults with limited English proficiency. Order from Center on Education and Training for Employment, 1900 Kenny Rd., Columbus, OH 43210.

SN7. *Equity from a Special Education Perspective.* Marc E. Hull. R and D Series no. 214H. Columbus, OH: National Center for Research in Vocational Education, 1982.

Examines equity in vocational education from the perspective of handicapped persons. Order from Center on Education and Training for Employment, 1900 Kenny Rd., Columbus, OH 43210.

SN8. *Profiles of Success: Twelve Exemplary Approaches to Serving Secondary Special Education Students Through the Carl D. Perkins Vocational Education Act.* John J. Gugerty et al. Madison, WI: University of Wisconsin, 1988.

Profiles the 12 top entrants in a four-step national competition. Includes evidence of each project's effectiveness, technical assistance available, mandates, exhibits, and additional information. Order from Center on Education and Work, University of Wisconsin-Madison, Department AM, 1025 W. Johnson St., Madison, WI 53706.

SN9. *Ready, Willing, and Able . . . : A Life and Career Planning Series for Women with Disabilities.* Carolyn Micchalski. Curriculum guide. Washington, DC: U.S. Department of Education, 1986.

Describes career and life planning activities developed for women with disabilities. Manual was developed to be used with the *Ready, Willing, and Able* videotape series, also available. Order from Vocational Studies Center, University of Wisconsin-Madison, 964 Educational Science Building, 1025 W. Johnson St., Madison, WI 53706.

SN10. "Sex Equity and Disabled Students." Jane Kratovil and Susan M. Bailey. *Theory into Practice* 25.4 (Autumn 1986): 250–56.

> Addresses the double jeopardy that confronts disabled students when bias and stereotyping based on gender and on disabling conditions interact.

SN11. *Still Puzzled about Educating Students with Disabilities: Vocational Preparation of Students with Disabilities.* Mary Gavin, ed. Madison, WI: University of Wisconsin, 1991.

> Helps vocational educators and other individuals provide appropriate vocational education for students with special needs by modifying vocational programs. Includes samples of modifications of instructional materials. A revised and updated version of *Puzzled about Educating Special Needs Students* (1980). Order from Center on Education and Work, University of Wisconsin-Madison, Department AM, 1025 W. Johnson St., Madison, WI 53706.

SN12. *Successful Vocational Rehabilitation of Persons with Learning Disabilities: Best Practices.* Madison, WI: University of Wisconsin, 1989.

> Details 83 of the best practices for dealing with learning disabled persons and provides an annotated bibliography of additional print and audiovisual materials. Order from Center on Education and Work, University of Wisconsin-Madison, Department AM, 1025 W. Johnson St., Madison, WI 53706.

SN13. *Taking the Next Step.* T. A. Ryan. Columbia, SC: University of South Carolina, 1988.

> Details the problems, needs, and issues facing female offenders and ex-offenders, including the emotional resistance and personal obstacles they face daily, and suggests strategies for overcoming them. Also offers thorough guidelines for establishing, operating, and evaluating an educational sup-

port program. Order from WEEA Publishing Center, 55 Chapel St., Suite 200, Newton, MA 02160.

SN14. *Women in Jail: Problems, Programs, and Resources.* Marjorie Brown Roy. Springfield, MA: YWCA, 1979. Describes the needs and problems of women in jail, diverse community-based program models, and the Female Offender Program in Hampden County, Massachusetts. Order from WEEA Publishing Center, 55 Chapel St., Suite 200, Newton, MA 02160.

21

Teaching (T)

T1. "Abolishing Misperceptions about Sex Equity in Education." Myra Sadker, David Sadker, and Susan S. Klein. *Theory into Practice* 25.4 (Autumn 1986): 221–26.

> Analyzes three misperceptions about gender equity in education: (1) that educational excellence and equity are not compatible and that one is achieved at the expense of the other, (2) that equity for women diverts resources from other groups in need, and (3) that sex equity has been achieved and that no problem exists anymore.

T2. *A-Gay-Yah*. Wathene Young. Curriculum guide. Tahlequah, OK: American Indian Resource Center, 1992.

> Contains classroom activities that create an awareness of and directly teach basic principles of gender equity. Includes quick-start activities and teaching lessons. Many lessons focus generally on Native American Culture. Order from WEEA Publishing Center, 55 Chapel St., Suite 200, Newton, MA 02160.

T3. *Beyond Pictures and Pronouns: Sexism in Teacher Education Textbooks*. Myra P. Sadker and David M. Sadker. Newton, MA: WEEA Publishing Center, 1979.

> Evaluates 24 best-selling teacher education textbooks published between 1973 and 1978, revealing pervasive and subtle sex bias. Examines the amount of content allocated to females, the treatment of women's experiences and contributions, and the presentation of sexism and sex differences. Provides data on racial and ethnic discrimination, suggestions for supplemental classroom activities, an annotated bibliography, and valuable guidelines for developing sex-fair textbooks. Order from 55 Chapel St., Suite 200, Newton, MA 02160.

T4. *Building Gender Fairness in Schools*. Beverly A. Stitt et al. Carbondale, IL: Southern Illinois University Press, 1988.

> Contains readings that summarize studies pertaining to sex bias in classroom interaction, curriculum materials, and the

classroom environment. Half of this teacher education textbook contains eleven units for use in developing gender-fair teaching competencies. Suitable for colleges of education and in-service teacher workshops. Order from Southern Illinois University at Carbondale, Carbondale, IL 62901.

T5.   *Checklist for Counteracting Race and Sex Bias in Educational Materials.* Martha P. Cotera. Newton, MA: WEEA Publishing Center, 1982.

Provides selected guidelines and checklists for selecting and evaluating curriculum materials for bilingual/multicultural education programs. Order from 55 Chapel St., Suite 200, Newton, MA 02160.

T6.   *A Checklist for Evaluating Materials.* Washington, DC: United States Government Printing Office, n.d.

Provides guidelines for evaluating educational materials for sex fairness. Order from Superintendent of Documents, Government Printing Office, Washington, DC 20402.

T7.   *Classroom Practices.* Anne Grant. Videocassette. Newton, MA: WEEA Publishing Center, 1979.

Considers ways to eliminate gender role stereotyping in the classroom. Part of the *Venture Beyond Stereotypes* program (GS). Order from 55 Chapel St., Suite 200, Newton, MA 02160.

T8.   *Color Our Children Carefully.* Sheryl Denbo et al. Washington, DC: American University, n.d.

Helps educators create and sustain effective schools. Includes statistical profiles, summaries of research findings, instructional and managerial strategies, and suggestions for identifying practitioner-oriented resources. Order from Mid-Atlantic Center for Race Equity, School of Education, American University, Washington, DC 20016.

T9.   *Educational Equity: Teaching, Learning, Achieving.* Sarah H. Mussett. Curriculum guide containing individual units. Stillwater, OK: Oklahoma State Board of Vocational and Technical Education, 1981.

Provides specific classroom strategies for promoting sex-fair education. Designed for use by state vocational education personnel to train teachers, administrators, and staff in the area of sex bias and gender role stereotyping. May be used by local classroom teachers to supplement existing materials on sex bias and gender role stereotyping in vocational education. Each unit includes performance objectives, suggested activities for teachers, information sheets, transparency masters, assignment sheets, job sheets, tests, and answers to tests and assignment sheets. Order from the Curriculum and Instructional Materials Center, Oklahoma State Board of Vocational and Technical Education, Stillwater, OK 74078.

T10.   *Equity in Physical Education*. Annie Clement and Betty Hartman. Newton, MA: WEEA Publishing Center, 1980.

Helps teachers design programs based on the abilities and interests of their particular students, regardless of their sex or grade level. Using the detailed checklist, teachers can observe and analyze students' motor performance and social interaction. Order from 55 Chapel St., Suite 200, Newton, MA 02160.

T11.   *Equity Lesson Plans*. Sharon Chester. Wichita, KS: KEDDS/LINK, n.d.

Compilation of lesson plans for various age groups. Order from Community Education Center, 1847 N. Chautauqua, Wichita, KS 67214.

T12.   *Evaluating Vocational and Career Education Media for Equity*. Software. Topeka, KS: Kansas State Department of Education, 1984.

Introduces and helps the user identify potential sources of bias in vocational and career education media and provides a means of rating vocational and career education media for equity. May be used to review films, filmstrips, slide/tape presentations, videocassettes, microcomputer software, audio recordings, and overhead transparency or picture sets. Order from 120 E. Tenth St., Topeka, KS 66612.

T13.   *Facing the Future*. Martha Matthews. Washington, DC: Council of Chief State School Officers Resource Center on Sex Equity, 1980.

Poses considerations for leaders in elementary and secondary education regarding education and equity for male and female students. Order from 400 N. Capitol St., NW, Suite 379, Washington, DC 20001.

T14. *Fair and Balanced Treatment of Minorities and Women.* Pamphlet. Cincinnati, OH: South-Western Publishing, 1976. Contains guidelines for the preparation of instructional materials by South-Western Publishing authors, editorial staff, and artists. Includes a section titled "Fair and Balanced Treatment—Language Usage and Content." Order from 5101 Madison Rd., Cincinnati, OH 45227.

T15. *Fair Play in the Classroom.* Charlotte Faris. Columbus, OH: Ohio Department of Education, 1982.
Covers the basic areas of equity. Provides an overview of fair classroom practices and suggested performance activities. Other modules are available. Order from Division of Vocational and Career Education, Ohio Department of Education, Columbus, OH 43216.

T16. "Finding Reality among the Myths: Why What You Thought about Sex Equity in Education Isn't So." Glen Harvey. *Phi Delta Kappan*, Mar. 1986, 509–12.
Explores myths that cloud the discussion of whether inequitable education has been laid to rest. The author argues that equity and excellence can be achieved. Part of the "Women in Education" series (T).

T17. "A Gender at Risk." Carol Shakeshaft. *Phi Delta Kappan*, Mar. 1986, 499–503.
Asserts that females still are not accorded equality of treatment or equality of outcome in most schools. The author qualifies the situation as a major crisis in education. Part of the "Women in Education" series.

T18. *Gender Issues in the Teaching of English.* Bruce Appleby and Nancy Mellin McCracken, eds. Portsmouth, NH: Boynton/Cook-Heinemann, 1992.
Contains various chapters about specific impacts of gender issues on teaching English. Includes "Psychological and So-

ciolinguistic Bases for Gender-Sensitive Teaching" and "A Bibliography for Gender Balancing the English Curriculum."

T19.   *A Guide to Educational Equity in Vocational Programs.* Pamela Crawford. Springfield, IL: Illinois State Board of Education, 1979.

Contains a checklist for recognizing and eliminating sex bias in instructional materials, suggestions for using biased materials in a nonbiased way, and guidelines for developing gender equity in the classroom. Order from Illinois State Curriculum Center, Sangamon State University, Springfield, IL 62794.

T20.   *Guidelines for Sex-Fair Vocational Education Materials.* Princeton, NJ: Women on Words and Images, 1978.

Helps vocational education teachers recognize and deal with sex biases contained in vocational education materials and helps students explore their own biases that result from their culture. Order from P.O. Box 2163, Princeton, NJ 08106.

T21.   *Guidelines for the Creative Use of Biased Materials in a Non-Biased Way.* Princeton, NJ: Women on Words and Images, 1978.

Helps vocational education teachers recognize and mitigate the effects of sex biases contained in vocational education materials. Meets the needs of teachers unable to replace expensive teaching materials that contain offensive biased concepts, pictures, and omission. Order from P.O. Box 2163, Princeton, NJ 08540.

T22.   *Handbook for Achieving Sex Equity Through Education.* Susan S. Klein. Baltimore, MD: Johns Hopkins University Press, 1985.

Compiles articles that describe key gender equity issues and make recommendations for achieving gender equity in and through education. Order from 2715 N. Charles St., Baltimore, MD 21218.

T23.   *Handbook of Training Activities to Combat Sexism in Education.* Mary M. Campbell and Robert W. Terry. Ann Arbor, MI: University of Michigan, n.d.

Contains structured exercises that combat sexism. For adults, but educators could use some of the activities with their students. Order from Program for Educational Opportunity, School of Education, University of Michigan, Ann Arbor, MI 48109.

T24. " 'I Have Always Worked': Elementary Schoolteaching as a Career." Sari Knopp Biklen. *Phi Delta Kappan*, Mar. 1986, 504–8.

Highlights the positive aspects of teaching young children. Part of the "Women in Education" series (T).

T25. *Implementing Guidelines*. Springfield, IL: Illinois State Board of Education, 1980.

Outlines guidelines for implementing gender equity in Illinois. Order from 100 N. First St., Springfield, IL 62777.

T26. *Implementing Project Awareness*. Beth Voorhees Wilke and C. David Beers. Arlington, VA: Superintendent of Public Instruction, 1977.

Reports on seven state education agencies participating in Project Awareness. Shares experiences and insights gained over their two-year implementation of a training program designed to increase awareness of sex bias and to encourage educators to initiate affirmative steps to achieve gender equity in education. Order from Office for Equal Education, Superintendent of Public Instruction, Arlington, VA 98223.

T27. "The Journey from Male-Defined to Gender-Balanced Education." Mary Thompson Tetreault. *Theory into Practice* 25.4 (Autumn 1986): 227–34.

Provides a retrospective look at the change in gender emphasis in education.

T28. *The New Plus: Creating a Positive, Sex-Fair Learning Environment*. Susan Jones Sears. OH: Ohio State University, 1984.

Provides specific strategies to help teachers develop positive, sex-fair climates in their classrooms. Teachers examine their current practices and attitudes through exercises and are challenged to implement new ones when appropriate. Order from Center for Sex Equity in Vocational Education, 123 Townshend Hall, 1885 Neil Ave., Columbus, OH 43210.

T29.   *Non-Sexist Teaching.* Myra Sadker, Dawn Thomas, and David Sadker. Washington, DC: Mid-Atlantic Center for Sex Equity, 1980.

> Helps educators see how biases may appear in teacher behavior and how they may be eliminated. Focuses on four patterns of sex bias in classroom interactions: sex segregation, classroom discipline, active teaching attention, and verbal evaluation. Order from 5010 Wisconsin Ave., NW, Suite 308, Washington, DC 20016.

T30.   "Preparing Teachers to Confront Sexism in Schools: A Competency-Based Approach." Myra Sadker and David Sadker. *Clearinghouse*, Oct. 1975, 57–61.

> Describes practical, specific steps toward becoming more sex-fair as a teacher.

T31.   *Preparing Women to Teach Non-Traditional Vocational Education.* Roslyn D. Kane. Columbus, OH: Ohio State University, 1978.

> Provides a model for retraining women teachers and skilled women to become teachers in traditionally male-dominated secondary vocational education. Order from ERIC Clearinghouse on Adult, Career, and Vocational Education, Center on Education and Training for Employment, 1900 Kenny Rd., Columbus, OH 43210.

T32.   *Resocializing Sex Roles: A Guide for Educators.* Elinor B. Waters. American Personnel and Guidance Association, 1980.

> Identifies developmental stages in women's and men's lives, gives guidelines for developing and evaluating educational programs, and views the problems and processes of social change.

T33.   *Sex Equity Handbook for Schools.* Myra Sadker and David Sadker. New York: Longman, 1982. Reprint. 1990.

> Collects information available on gender equity in the schools into a practical form that teachers can apply in their classrooms. Includes field-tested strategies for detecting and

combating gender role stereotyping in curriculum materials
and classroom interaction, specific lesson plans and unit activities that teachers can draw on as models, a thorough
treatment of the harmful impact that gender role stereotyping has on males as well as females, and a comprehensive,
up-to-date resource directory of organizations providing materials and training assistance on the issue of gender equity.
Order from 19 W. 44th St., New York, NY 10036.

T34.   "Sexism in the Classroom: From Grade School to
Graduate School." Myra Sadker and David Sadker. *Phi Delta
Kappan*, Mar. 1986, 512–15.

Contends that classrooms at all levels are characterized by a
general environment of inequity and that bias in classroom
interaction inhibits student achievement. Provides suggestions for change. Part of the "Women in Education" series
(T).

T35.   "Strategies for Achieving Sex Equity in Education."
Glen Harvey and Leslie F. Hergert. *Theory into Practice* 25.4
(Autumn 1986): 290–99.

Identifies strategies for achieving and maintaining gender
equity in education. Includes an analysis of the change process as it relates to implementing gender equity in education.

T36.   "Teachers: The Key to Unlocking Sex Equity." Charlotte J. Farris. *VocEd*, Apr. 1980, 18–20.

Considers what teachers can do to promote gender equity.

T37.   *Title IX—Teacher's Role: Identifying and Overcoming
Sex Bias.* Martha Matthews and Shirley McCune. Denver, CO:
Colorado Department of Education, 1980.

Helps educational personnel and interested citizens implement Title IX. Intended for all instructional personnel.

T38.   "Women in Education." *Phi Delta Kappan*, Mar. 1986,
499–526.

Contains several articles addressing specific problems for
females in educational environments.

22 Vocational Education (VE)

VE1. *Access to Quality Vocational Education: A Sex Equity Perspective.* Rebecca S. Douglas. Paper prepared for the National Assessment of Vocational Education, U.S. Department of Education, 1986.

> Assesses vocational educators' accomplishments during the past decade toward reducing gender role stereotyping and improving women's access to high quality vocational education. Discusses remaining obstacles to gender equity, unresolved issues, and recommendations for future research. Order from Illinois State Curriculum Center, Sangamon State University, Springfield, IL 62794.

VE2. *Analysis of Michigan's Sex Equity Efforts in Vocational Education with Recommendations.* Paper. Lansing, MI: State Advisory Council for Vocational Education, 1985.

> Explains the importance of gender equity in vocational education, gives the historical background leading to legislation requiring gender equity, presents findings from a review of the state's efforts to reduce gender role stereotyping in vocational education, and makes recommendations for the state to improve its gender equity program and effectively use new resources under the 1984 act.

VE3. *Annual Status Report on Female and Male Students and Employees in Vocational Education.* Raleigh, NC: North Carolina Department of Public Instruction, 1984–85.

> Outlines North Carolina's efforts toward achieving gender equity in vocational education. Order from Sex Equity/Division of Vocational Education, North Carolina Department of Public Instruction, Raleigh, NC 27603.

VE4. *Arkansas Female-Male Students and Employees in Vocational Education.* Little Rock, AR: Arkansas Department of Education, 1985.

> Contains 1984–85 status report. Order from Vocational and Technical Education Division, Sex Equity Program, Arkansas Department of Education, Little Rock, AR 72205.

VE5. "Building Fairness in Illinois." Janice Cluck, Beverly Stitt, and Heidi Perreault. *Workplace Education*, May/June 1986, 5.

> Describes the Illinois Building Fairness project, including major activities and funded minigrants.

VE6. *Civil Rights in Vocational Education: Annual Report 1984–85.* Springfield, IL: Illinois State Board of Education, 1985.

> Contains progress report. Order from Department of Vocational, Technical, and Adult Education, 100 N. First St., Springfield, IL 62777.

VE7. *A Collection of Papers from a Symposium on Sex Equity in Vocational Education: Summary of Research.* James A. Knight. Columbus, Ohio: Department of Education, 1983.

> Contains papers regarding gender equity programs in vocational education. Topics include sex bias of state FFA degree applications, nontraditional and traditional completers' attitudes, and recruitment of nontraditional male and female students. Order from the Division of Vocational Education, 65 S. Front St., Columbus, Ohio 43215.

VE8. *Employment Policies: Looking to the Year 2000.* Washington, DC: National Alliance of Business, 1986.

> Addresses possible mismatches that may arise between workplace needs and work force capabilities in the next 10 to 15 years and gives suggestions for resolving the differences. Order from 1015 15th St., NW, Washington, DC 20005.

VE9. *Equity from a Large City Director's Perspective.* Irving Kovarsky. R and D Series no. 214P. Columbus, OH: National Center for Research in Vocational Education, 1982.

> Traces legislative developments that favorably and unfavorably affect employment equity. Order from Center on Education and Training for Employment, 1900 Kenny Rd., Columbus, OH 43210.

VE10. *Equity from a Public Administration Perspective.* Yearn H. Choi. R and D Series no. 214C. Columbus, OH: National Center for Research in Vocational Education, 1982.

Traces the history of equity in public policy and relates it to vocational education. Order from Center on Education and Training for Employment, 1900 Kenny Rd., Columbus, OH 43210.

VE11. *Equity from a Racial/Ethnic Perspective.* Samuel D. Proctor. R and D Series no. 214J. Columbus, OH: National Center for Research in Vocational Education, 1982.

Provides an orientation to the current equity status of minority youth. Order from Center on Education and Training for Employment, 1900 Kenny Rd., Columbus, OH 43210.

VE12. *Equity from a Sex Fairness Perspective.* Nancy Smith Evans. R and D Series no. 214F. Columbus, OH: National Center for Research in Vocational Education, 1982.

Concentrates on the challenges and responsibilities of gender equity coordinators and makes numerous suggestions for the successful implementation of gender equity legislation. Order from Center on Education and Training for Employment, 1900 Kenny Rd., Columbus, OH 43210.

VE13. *Equity from a Sociological Perspective.* Jerome J. Salomone. R and D Series no. 214L. Columbus, OH: National Center for Research in Vocational Education, 1982.

Examines equity as a theoretical subject predicated on an existential philosophy. Order from Center on Education and Training for Employment, 1900 Kenny Rd., Columbus, OH 43210.

VE14. *Equity from a State Administrator's Perspective.* Geneva Fletcher. R and D Series no. 214G. Columbus, OH: National Center for Research in Vocational Education, 1982.

Discusses legislative requirements of Title II of the Education Amendments of 1976 and the responsibilities of state directors of vocational education for achieving equity. Order from Center on Education and Training for Employment, 1900 Kenny Rd., Columbus, OH 43210.

VE15. *Equity from a Vocational District Director's Perspective.* Richard N. Adams. R and D Series no. 214A. Columbus, OH: National Center for Research in Vocational Education, 1982.

Considers equity from the perspective of an administrator of a vocational education center serving rural high school and adult students. Order from Center on Education and Training for Employment, 1900 Kenny Rd., Columbus, OH 43210.

VE16. *Equity from a Vocational Teacher Educator's Perspective.* Clyde W. Welter. R and D Series no. 214Q. Columbus, OH: National Center for Research in Vocational Education, 1982.

Considers equity from the perspective of teacher educators whose responsibilities include providing preservice and inservice training for the preparation of vocational teachers, performing research, and providing graduate education. Order from Center on Education and Training for Employment, 1900 Kenny Rd., Columbus, OH 43210.

VE17. *Equity from an Aging Specialist's Perspective.* Alan N. Sheppard. R and D Series no. 214O. Columbus, OH: National Center for Research in Vocational Education, 1982.

Begins with a comprehensive assessment of demographic trends and their impact on vocational education and employment opportunities for older adults. Order from Center for Education and Training for Employment, 1900 Kenny Rd., Columbus, OH 43210.

VE18. *Equity Status Report: Vocational Education, State of Montana.* Raymond D. Brown and Gene Christiansen. Helena, MT: Department of Vocational Education Services, 1984.

Reports on the annual status of female and male students in vocational education and displaced homemaker programs designed to eliminate sex bias, stereotyping, and discrimination. Order from Office of Public Instruction, State Capitol, Helena, MT 59620.

VE19. "The Equity Study: Results and Recommendations." Laurie R. Harrison. *VocEd*, Apr. 1980, 39–42.

Considers whether progress is being made toward achieving gender equity in education and highlights necessary requirements for successful programs.

VE20. *Evaluation of the National Sex Equity Demonstration Project.* Bernadine Evans Stake, Robert E. Stake, Laura Morgan, and James Pearsol. Miami, FL: National Sex Equity Demonstration Project at Broward County, 1983.

Contains the final report of the project.

VE21. *Factors Related to Underrepresentation of Women in Vocational Education Administration: A Literature Review.* Ellen Bowers and Judythe Hummel. Columbus, OH: National Center for Research in Vocational Education, 1979.

Documents factors relating to the underrepresentation of women in vocational education administration, establishes a sound data base for dissemination to the field, and encourages other project and program efforts toward increasing women's representation. Order from Center on Education and Training for Employment, 1900 Kenny Rd., Columbus, OH 43210.

VE22. *Forum for Change.* Toni Moynihan. Corpus Christi, TX: Education Service Center, 1985.

Reports the major accomplishments of the Forum for Change equity project in Texas.

VE23. *Fostering Sex Fairness in Vocational Education: Strategies for Administrators.* JoAnn M. Steiger and Sue H. Schlesinger. Columbus, OH: National Center for Research in Vocational Education, 1979.

Provides for vocational education administrators an overview of gender equity issues and alternative strategies for action. Order from Center on Education and Training for Employment, 1900 Kenny Rd., Columbus, OH 43210.

VE24. *Future Influences on Vocational Education.* Booklet. Columbus, OH: National Center for Research in Vocational Education, 1985.

Helps planners and policymakers respond to changes in technology and in the makeup of the work force. In this transition period, it is difficult to know how best to prepare young people and to retrain adults for rewarding employment in a future whose structure is dimly perceivable. This booklet is designed to assist in the decision-making process. Order from Center on Education and Training for Employment, 1900 Kenny Rd., Columbus, OH 43210.

VE25. *Futures Unlimited II: Expanding Your Horizons in Technical and Vocational Education.* Videocassette. New Brunswick, NJ: State University of New Jersey, 1986.

> Provides as role models women who have pursued training and careers in technology-related fields. 29 min. Order from Consortium for Educational Equity, Rutgers, Kilmer Campus 4090, New Brunswick, NJ 08903.

VE26. *Georgia's Students and Employees in Vocational Education.* Ann Lary and Barbara Landay. Atlanta, GA: Georgia Department of Education, 1985.

> Contains 1980–84 status report.

VE27. *Guidelines for Equity Issues in Technology Education.* Donna Koppi Boben. Reston, VA: International Technology Education Association, 1985.

> Includes strategies to help the International Technology Education Association work toward achieving race and gender equity through technology education. Designed to help the user become aware of sex-fair and race-fair language and visuals and of techniques to portray women and people of all races equitably in their roles. Order from 1914 Association Dr., Reston, VA 22091.

VE28. *The Impact of Early Work Experience on the Vocational Development of Young Women Workers.* Jane Levine Powers. Ithaca, NY: Cornell University, 1986.

> Examines the influence of early work experience on the socialization of female adolescents to the work world. Focuses on young women who leave high school intending to enter the labor force immediately and examines whether their early work experiences (prior to high school graduation) influence their vocational choices and aspirations, vocational planning abilities, and early labor market experiences after graduation. Results suggest that early work experience has a significant impact on adolescent vocational development. Order from Human Development and Family Studies, Cornell University, Ithaca, NY 14853.

VE29. *Increasing Sex Equity.* Arlington, VA: Institute for Women's Concerns, Dec. 1980.

Contains a report of the National Advisory Council on Vocational Education and the National Advisory Council on Women's Educational Programs. Examines whether the implementation of the 1976 Vocational Education Amendments on gender equity in vocational education have resulted in equitable access to and benefit from the nation's vocational education system by women and men, girls and boys. Order from 1018 Wilson Blvd., Arlington, VA 22209.

VE30. *Network Project Implementation Guides.* Sally Vaughn and Jim Mahrt. Wayne, MI: Wayne County Intermediate School District, 1986.

Contains a series of practical, how-to guides for implementing gender equity strategies in vocational education. Provides detailed implementation steps and forms for conducting activities and includes tips for success. The 11 guides are "How to Create and/or Revise a Slide/Tape Presentation for Vocational Education," "How to Create and/or Revise Brochures for Vocational Education," "How to Conduct a Materials Review for Sex Bias," "How to Conduct Awareness in Services for School Staff," "How to Identify and Use Nontraditional Role Models," "How to Organize and Conduct Nontraditional Career Days," "How to Use Vocational Interest Inventories in Sex Affirmative and Equitable Ways," "Using Support Groups to Retain Nontraditional Vocational Students," "How to Implement a Public Information Program for Vocational Education," "How a Career Center Can Promote Sex-Equity Activities into All Areas of the Curriculum," and "A Model Recruitment Presentation for Nontraditional Vocational Students." Order from Network Project, P.O. Box 807, Wayne, MI 48184.

VE31. *Network Project Material User Guides.* Wayne, MI: Wayne County Intermediate School District, n.d.

Includes information on type of material, recommended grade level and use, and time required for use, and gives suggestions for implementation. User guides for the most frequently requested gender equity materials are available from Michigan State University Vocational Education Resource Center. Order from Network Project, P.O. Box 807, Wayne, MI 48184.

VE32. *Professional Development Programs for Sex Equity in Vocational Education.* Mary Ellen Verheydon-Hilliard. Columbus, OH: National Center for Research in Vocational Education, 1979.

Reviews state-of-the-art professional development programs as they relate to gender equity in vocational education. Order from Center on Education and Training for Employment, 1900 Kenny Rd., Columbus, OH 43210.

VE33. "Programs for Women and Girls." *VocEd*, Mar. 1987, 38–40.

Describes some existing programs for single parents, battered women, young women, and teen parents.

VE34. *Project Equity . . . Whose Progress?* Springfield, IL: Illinois State Board of Education, 1986.

Contains a resource bibliography that includes resources for parents, educators, and business/industry leaders. Order from Department of Adult, Vocational, and Technical Education, 100 N. First St., Springfield, IL 62777.

VE35. *Promising Programs for Sex-Fair Vocational Education.* San Francisco, CA: Far West Laboratory for Educational Research and Development, 1981.

Documents 47 promising approaches to sex-fair vocational education training throughout the U.S.

VE36. "Sex Equity: Challenge of Change." *Workplace Education*, 4.4 (May/June 1986).

Contains several related articles.

VE37. *Sex Equity in High Technology Vocational Education.* Emily Daxton. Curriculum guide. Pueblo, CO: Pueblo Community College, 1987.

Provides strategies and techniques for increasing sex fairness in vocational education for both men and women. Focuses on high-tech careers.

VE38. *Sex Equity in Vocational Education.* Videocassette. Columbus, OH: Ohio Department of Education, 1987.

Provides an overview of the need for gender equity in vocational education. Designed for educators. Order from Division of Vocational and Career Education, 65 Front St., Columbus, OH 43266.

VE39. *The Special Vocational Education Needs of Women.* Rene C. Kane and Constance W. Cline. Springfield, IL: Illinois State Board of Education, 1978.

Describes the development of the Expanding Career Horizons curriculum, the film *When I Grow Up* . . ., and the curriculum dissemination workshops, and assesses the impact of the project. Order from Department of Adult, Vocational, and Technical Education, 100 N. First St., Springfield, IL 62777.

VE40. *Statewide Leadership Identification Program.* Madison, WI: Wisconsin Board of Vocational, Technical, and Adult Education, 1983.

Describes 23 projects completed by participants in the Wisconsin statewide Leadership Identification Program, 1982–83. Order from 4802 Sheboygan Ave., 7th Floor, P.O. Box 7874, Madison, WI 53707.

VE41. *Status Report on Male and Female Students and Employees in Illinois Vocational Education.* Springfield, IL: Illinois State Board of Education, 1980.

Contains data on program enrollments by sex, occupational areas, and educational levels of students and employees. Order from Department of Adult, Vocational, and Technical Education, 100 N. First St., Springfield, IL 62777.

VE42. *Title IX—The World of Work: Title IX and Sex Equity.* Martha Matthews and Shirley McCune. Denver, CO: Colorado Department of Education, 1980.

Contains a Title IX/Sex Equity training model designed to help educational personnel and interested citizens implement Title IX. Intended for administrators, counselors, and teachers from vocational education programs. Includes trainer's and participants' manuals.

VE43. "To Be an Administrator, and a Woman." Geneva Fletcher. *VocEd*, Apr. 1980, 31–33.

Presents the author's view of women in vocational education administration.

VE44. *Try It, You'll Like It!* Martha Matthews and Shirley McCune. Washington, DC: National Foundation for the Improvement of Education, 1978.

> Includes readings and activities that introduce secondary students to nonsexist vocational education. Order from Resource Center on Sex Roles in Education, 1201 16th St., NW, Washington, DC 20036.

VE45. *Update: A Guide for Vocational Education Sex Equity Personnel.* Louise Vetter. Columbus, OH: National Center for Research in Vocational Education, 1986.

> Lists the purposes of the Carl D. Perkins Vocational Education Act and the requirements of the state plan as they relate to the gender equity coordinator. Order from Center on Education and Training for Employment, 1900 Kenny Rd., Columbus, OH 43210.

VE46. *Vocational Education Sex Equity Strategies.* Louise Vetter, Carolyn Burkhardt, and Judith Sechler. R and D Series no. 144. Columbus, OH: National Center for Research in Vocational Education, 1978.

> Provides strategies and techniques for increasing sex fairness in vocational education. Order from Center on Education and Training for Employment, 1900 Kenny Rd., Columbus, OH 43210.

VE47. *Vocational Sex Equity Project Abstracts, 1985–86.* Elizabeth M. Hawa. Richmond, VA: Virginia Department of Education, 1986.

> Compiles abstracts for 37 projects funded through the Carl D. Perkins Vocational Education Act that serve single parents and homemakers, teen parents, and women in nontraditional careers in Virginia.

VE48. "What to Do about Those Biased Materials." Marla Peterson and Louise Vetter. *VocEd*, Apr. 1980, 34–38.

> Contains four teaching/learning activities for use in vocational classes and gives suggestions for evaluating materials for sex bias.

VE49. *Youth 2000*. Washington, DC: National Alliance of Business, 1986.

Focuses on complex and challenging issues facing today's youth, such as gender roles, a changing workplace, and new career choices, and begins to develop an agenda for individual, institutional, and collaborative action at the federal, state, and community level. Reports on a June 1986 national leadership meeting. Order from 1015 15th St., NW, Suite 500, Washington, DC 20005.

23 Women's Studies (WS)

WS1. *America's Working Women.* Rosalyn Baxandall, Linda Gordon, and Susan Reverby, eds. Santa Rosa, CA: National Women's History Project, 1976.

Contains contemporary essays, diaries, union records, letters, songs, social workers' reports, statistics, and photographs that chronicle the lives of women laborers of virtually all cultures, races, and work force areas from 1600 to the present. Order from P.O. Box 3716, Santa Rosa, CA 95402.

WS2. *The Anatomy of Oppression: A Feminist Analysis of Psychotherapy.* Joyce Jennings Walstedt. Pittsburgh, PA: Know, 1971.

Considers why a feminist-oriented psychotherapy is needed. Order from P.O. Box 86031, Pittsburgh, PA 15221.

WS3. *Appalachian Women.* Sharon B. Lord and Carolyn Patton-Crowder. Newton, MA: WEEA Publishing Center, 1979.

Focuses on the experiences of women in the Appalachian mountains. Examples of their poetry, music, and prose provide insight into these women's experiences. Part of *The Female Experience in America* package (WS). Order from 55 Chapel St., Suite 200, Newton, MA 02160.

WS4. *Beauty Bound.* Rita Freeman. Lexington, MA: Lexington Books, 1986.

Exposes the myth of female beauty. Drawing on her experience as a clinical psychologist, the author shows how the power of beauty places women on a pedestal, while the burden of beauty demeans them as inadequate. Does not condemn people for trying to look their best, but questions how and why we all become caught up in the pageantry of feminine display. Order from D.C. Heath and Company, Lexington Books, Lexington, MA 02173.

WS5. *Being a Woman, in a Man's World, Doing Unmanly Things, for, but Apart from, Men.* Robert A. Zuckerman. Columbus, OH: Ohio State University, 1980.

Considers various avenues women's lives may take through simulation exercise. Order from Ohio Distributive Education Materials Lab, 123 Townshend Hall, 1885 Neil Ave., Columbus, OH 43210.

WS6. *Beyond Sugar and Spice*. Caryl Rivers, Rosalind Barnett, and Grace Baruch. New York: Ballantine Books, 1983.

Contains a comprehensive study of the forces that shape a woman's ability to survive and succeed in a rapidly changing world.

WS7. *The Black Female Experience in America*. Joanna Allman et al. Newton, MA: WEEA Publishing Center, 1979.

Traces the experiences that have shaped today's African-American woman. Explores African-American feminism, the strengths of the African-American family, and the dynamics of being a minority person in America. Part of *The Female Experience in America* package (WS). Order from 55 Chapel St., Suite 200, Newton, MA 02160.

WS8. *A Closer Look at Mentoring*. New York: Catalyst, 1986.

Discusses using formalized and informal mentoring to promote women's advancement in organizations. Order from 250 Park Ave. South, New York, NY 10003.

WS9. *The Criminal Justice System and Women*. Barbara Raffel Price. New York: Clark Boardman Collogham, 1982.

Provides a comprehensive overview of the treatment of women in the criminal justice system—as offenders, as victims of crime, and as working members of the system. Order from 375 Hudson St., New York, NY 10014.

WS10. *The Effectiveness of Women's Studies Teaching*. Nancy M. Porter. Washington, DC: National Institute of Education, 1980.

Examines the teaching of women's studies at the college level. Order from Social Processes/Women's Research Team, National Institute of Education, Mail Stop 7, 1200 19th Street, NW, Washington, DC 20280.

WS11. *The Elimination of Sexism in University Environments*. Linda Forrest, Kathy Hotelling, and Linda Kuk. Paper presented at the second annual symposium of Student Development Through Campus Ecology, Pingree Park, CO, 1984.

Describes the developmental differences between males and females, current campus environments and their effect on women's development, and an ideal campus environment established to nurture and support women's development. Incorporates an understanding of female development and female values into suggested intervention methods for reducing sexism on campuses.

WS12. *Equity from an Anthropological Perspective.* Henrietta Schwartz. R and D Series no. 214M. Columbus, OH: National Center for Research in Vocational Education, 1982.

Focuses on issues related to the cultural aspects of gender equity and schooling in American society and begins with a framework of assumptions that relates the discipline of anthropology to concepts of equity. Order from Center on Education and Training for Employment, 1900 Kenny Rd., Columbus, OH 43210.

WS13. *Equity Lessons.* Ida Kravitz. Newton, MA: WEEA Publishing Center, 1982.

Provides guidelines for setting up a systemwide women's studies program in primary and secondary schools. Contains two books: *Equity Lessons for Elementary School*, which contains activities for grade school children that reveal the importance of feelings, friendship, and language; and *Equity Lessons for Secondary School*, which tackles such difficult matters as personal assumptions, the ERA, and the meanings of the lives of activist women. Each book contains guidelines for selecting nonsexist books and other instructional aids. Order from 55 Chapel St., Suite 200, Newton, MA 02160.

WS14. *The Female Experience in America.* Sharon B. Lord et al. 4 vols. Newton, MA: WEEA Publishing Center, 1979.

Forces students to rethink their perceptions about individual and societal behavior. Contains the volumes *Understanding Sex Roles and Moving Beyond* (GS); *The Female Experience in America: Development, Counseling, and Career Issues*; *The Black Female Experience in America*; and *Appalachian Women* (WS). Order from 55 Chapel St., Suite 200, Newton, MA 02160.

WS15. *The Female Experience in America: Development, Counseling, and Career Issues.* Sharon B. Lord et al. Newton, MA: WEEA Publishing Center, 1979.

> Explores female socialization and the development of careers and life-styles. First examines women in counseling and offers guidelines for bias-free treatment. Then explores ways to counsel women in crisis. Part of the *Female Experience in America* package (WS). Order from 55 Chapel St., Suite 200, Newton, MA 02160.

WS16. *Female Offenders: Correctional Afterthoughts.* Robert R. Ross. Jefferson, NC: McFarland and Company, 1986.

> Reviews published literature on programs for juvenile and adult programming for females, the effectiveness of various programs, correctional services for women, and the implications for policy formation, program development, and research.

WS17. *Female Student Participation at Illinois Public Community Colleges.* Springfield, IL: Illinois Community College Board, 1987.

> Analyzes the enrollment and program completion of female students in Illinois public community colleges using data on the Illinois Community College Board computerized data system for fiscal years 1984–87. Data is updated periodically. Order from 509 S. Sixth St., Room 400, Springfield, IL 62701.

WS18. "The Feminization of Poverty: More Women are Getting Poorer." Vicky Cahan. *Business Week*, 28 Jan. 1985, 84–85.

> Gives statistics that show an increase in the number of women who live below poverty level. Included in the *Women at Work* series (WS).

WS19. *Fulfilling the Mandate: Eighth Annual Report for Fiscal Year 1982.* Betty Cordoba. Washington, DC: United States Department of Education, 1983.

> Describes the 1982 activities of the National Advisory Council on Women's Educational Programs and the results of

the Women's Educational Equity Act program evaluation. Includes recommendations for educational equity options. Order from National Advisory Council on Women's Educational Programs, 1832 M St., NW, Washington, DC 20005.

WS20. *The Heart of Excellence: Equal Opportunities and Educational Reform.* Washington, DC: Project on Equal Education Rights, 1987.

Discusses the relationship between educational equity and excellence and gives recommendations for equity reforms. Order from 99 Hudson St., 12th Floor, New York, NY 10013.

WS21. *Hers.* Nancy R. Newhouse, ed. New York: Villard Books, 1985.

Contains a collection of 65 essays that have appeared in the *New York Times* column entitled "Hers." Each essay was chosen for the perspective it brings to various aspects of women's lives.

WS22. *The Hidden Discriminator: Color, Sex, and Race Bias in Educational Research.* Patricia B. Campbell. Groton, MA: Campbell-Kibler Associates, 1989.

Provides an in-depth examination of stereotypes and bias in educational research and explores the hidden effects of bias on decision making and program design in education. Order from WEEA Publishing Center, 55 Chapel St., Suite 200, Newton, MA 02160.

WS23. *The Impact of Women on American Education.* Linda K. Kerber. Newton, MA: WEEA Publishing Center, 1983.

Provides information about issues of sexism and the opportunity to develop skills in approaches to alleviating this problem in schools. One of six curricular units developed by the Non-Sexist Teacher Education Project. Designed for use in preservice teacher education programs. Order from 55 Chapel St., Suite 200, Newton, MA 02160.

WS24. *The Impact of Women's Studies on the Campus and the Disciplines.* Florence Howe and Paul Lauter. Washington, DC: National Institute of Education, 1980.

Examines women's studies across disciplines at the college level. Order from Social Processes/Women's Research Team, National Institute of Education, Mail Stop 7, 1200 19th St., NW, Washington, DC 20208.

WS25. *Inequality of Sacrifice: The Impact of the Reagan Budget on Women.* Washington, DC: National Women's Law Center, 1984.

Analyzes the impact of the federal budget on women that was proposed by the Reagan administration's ad hoc Coalition on Women and the Budget. Includes a grass roots organizing kit. Order from 1616 P St., NW, Washington, DC 20036.

WS26. *Job Options: First Offender Women . . . A Pre-Trial Intervention Program.* Marilyn B. Goldman. Filmstrip. Washington, DC: U.S. Department of Education, 1979.

Encourages and increases awareness of the special problems of women offenders and provides guidance on how to work toward solutions. Describes a pretrial intervention program. Includes a manual. Order from WEEA Publishing Center, 55 Chapel St., Suite 200, Newton, MA 02160.

WS27. *A Lesser Life.* Sylvia Ann Hewlett. New York: William Morrow and Company, 1986.

Compares the lives of European women and American women. European women enjoy job-protected maternity leave, subsidized child care, child allowances, lower divorce rates, and a narrowing wage gap, but American women have only a precarious security as workers, wives, and mothers. Despite their legendary claim to power and privilege, women in the U.S. actually face a bad and deteriorating economic reality. To better understand this paradox, Hewlett explores the "aberrant fifties," the cult of motherhood, radical feminism, the battle to ratify the ERA, and government policies toward women and children.

WS28. "The Myth of Women's Liberation." Sylvia Ann Hewlett. *Working Mother*, May 1986, 19–20.

Examines what American women have gained and what they have given up. Drawn from *A Lesser Life* (WS).

WS29. *NOW's 20th Anniversary.* Videocassette. Los Angeles, CA: Peg Yorkin Productions, 1986.

Takes a serious, yet humorous, look at women's lives over the past 20 years through the use of archival film, film essays, short landmark statements, and musical numbers with many stars. Order from 8105 W. 3rd St., Suite 1, Los Angeles, CA 90048.

WS30. "O Brave New Curriculum: Feminism and the Future of Liberal Arts." Leslie R. Wolfe. *Theory into Practice* 25.4 (Autumn 1986): 284–89.

Considers the reform of the liberal arts curriculum.

WS31. *A Parent's Wish for Her Daughter.* Gabrielle Burton. Pittsburgh, PA: Know, n.d.

Describes some parents' hopes for positive futures for their daughters' lives. Order from P.O. Box 86031, Pittsburgh, PA 15221.

WS32. *Re-Entry Women Involved in Women's Studies.* Blanche Glassman Hersh. Washington, DC: National Institute of Education, 1980.

Describes the impact that women returning to school has on women's studies' programs. Order from Social Processes/ Women's Research Team, National Institute of Education, Mail Stop 7, 1200 19th St., NW, Washington, DC 20280.

WS33. *The Relationship Between Women's Studies, Career Development, and Vocational Choice.* Christine E. Bose and Janet Priest-Jones. Washington, DC: U.S. Government Printing Office, n.d.

Reviews the literature on the relationship of women's studies to career development and vocational outcomes and defines needs and outlines strategies for future research in this area. Order from Superintendent of Documents, 725 N. Capitol St., NW, Washington, DC 20402.

WS34. *Sending the Right Signals: A Training Program about Dealing with Sexual Harassment.* Patricia Mitchell. Videocassette. Jersey City, NJ: Jersey City State College, 1990.

Employs television personalities to help combat and prevent sexual harassment. Explores situations depicting sexual harassment at work and at school and gives techniques to help deal effectively with sexual harassment when it occurs. Order from Illinois State Curriculum Center, Sangamon State University, Springfield, IL 62794.

WS35. *Sourcebook of Measures of Women's Educational Equity.* Beverly J. Parks et al. Newton, MA: WEEA Publishing Center, 1982.

> Contains a clear, easy-to-use format for evaluating educational equity programs. Includes questionnaires, rating scales, inventories, interviews, and checklists. Order from 55 Chapel St., Suite 200, Newton, MA 02160.

WS36. *The State-by-State Survey of the Status of Women and Girls in America's Schools.* Washington, DC: Project on Equal Education Rights, 1986.

> Lists levels of access and achievement opportunities for females throughout America. Order from 99 Hudson St., 12th Floor, New York, NY 10013.

WS37. "An Undeserved Gap." Laurel Leff. *Working Women,* Apr. 1984, 28.

> Discusses a study from the University of Michigan's Institute of Social Research that reveals that differences between men and women in education, work experience, work continuity, self-imposed work restrictions on job locations and hours, and absenteeism account for only one-third of the wage gap between white women and white men and one-quarter of the gap between African-American women and white men. More accountable for the gap are women's occupational positions and the kind of training they receive in them.

WS38. *The United National Decade for Women, 1976–1985: Employment in the United States.* Washington, DC: U.S. Department of Labor, 1985.

> Assesses the progress women have made in employment and considers how to continue to build on those gains in the future. Report for the World Conference on the United Nations Decade for Women, 1976–85. Order from U.S. Department of Labor, Office of the Secretary, Women's

Bureau, 200 Constitution Ave., NW, Washington, DC 20210.

WS39. *WEAL's Agenda for Women's Economic Equity, 1985–86.* Washington, DC: Women's Equity Action League, 1985.

Analyzes women's economic status using the latest available data and gives specific proposals for reform. Completed annually. Order from 1250 I St., NW, Washington, DC 20005.

WS40. *Women in America.* Fort Worth, TX: Sperry and Hutchinson, 1976.

Answers questions about the achievements of women in America. Order from Consumer Affairs Department, 2900 W. Seminary Dr., Fort Worth, TX 76133.

WS41. *Women in Government.* Poster. Brooklyn, NY: TABS Aids for Equal Education, n.d.

Depicts a U.S. Flag as a chart comparing numbers of male (red stripes) and female (white stripes) members of congress, senators, supreme court justices, governors, local elected officials, and voters. Includes a quiz on women in government and a lesson plan on attitudes regarding a woman running for president. Order from 744 Carroll St., Brooklyn, NY 11215.

WS42. *Women's History Curriculum Guide.* Santa Rosa, CA: National Women's History Project, 1985.

Helps develop classroom activities, pattern puppets and paper dolls, and produce research and discussion questions. For grades K–12. All these cross-cultural materials may be reproduced for classroom use and are adaptable for social studies, ethnic studies, and history units. Order from P.O. Box 3716, Santa Rosa, CA 95402.

WS43. "Women's Rights vs. Fetal Rights Looms as Thorny and Divisive Issue." Alan L. Otten. *Wall Street Journal*, 12 Apr. 1985, 29.

Addresses the question of whether the government should, or constitutionally can, intervene to protect the fetus against a negligent mother.

WS44. *Women's Studies as a Catalyst for Faculty Development.* Elizabeth Ness Nelson. Washington, DC: National Institute of Education, 1980.

> Examines the extent to which women's studies has been involved in faculty development activities. Order from Social Processes/Women's Research Team, National Institute of Education, Mail Stop 7, 1200 19th St., NW, Washington, DC 20280.

WS45. *Women's Studies Graduates.* Elaine Reuben and Mary Jo Boehm Strauss. Washington, DC: National Institute of Education, 1980.

> Surveys research- and data-gathering needs among women's studies graduates. Order from Social Processes/Women's Research Team, National Institute of Education, Mail Stop 7, 1200 19th St., NW, Washington, DC 20280.

WS46. *Women's Studies in the Community Colleges.* Allana Elovson. Washington, DC: National Institute of Education, 1980.

> Reviews the literature on women's studies programs in community colleges and makes recommendations for future action. Order from Social Processes/Women's Research Team, National Institute of Education, Mail Stop 7, 1200 19th St., NW, Washington, DC 20280.

WS47. *The World's Women.* Washington, DC: Population Reference Bureau, 1986.

> Helps teachers raise their students' awareness of the important issues from *The United National Decade for Women, 1976–1985: Employment in the United States* (WS). Designed as a reading and activity booklet for students. Order from Population Reference Bureau, 777 14th St., NW, Washington, DC 20005.

INDEX

INDEX

Each resource is described just once in an entry in the bibliography. The entry is located under the bibliographical category that most clearly reflects the resource's primary focus. However, many resources fit into more than one category. In the index, the reader can locate a category of particular interest and find a listing of the entry codes of all resources pertaining to that category. A category entitled Secondary Education has been added to the index to help high school personnel locate relevant materials.

Agriculture and industry
(AI1–AI18): VE27

Business (B1–B32): CG52,
CP4, CP12, D22, D25,
DH13, FW10, FW42,
GS36, GS60, NT25,
NT29, NT49, NT84,
R10, WS8

Career guidance (CG1–
CG55): AI1, AI2, B5,
B16, CP17, DH1, DH7,
DH10, DH12, DH18,
DH19, EE13, EE19,
FW38, GS1, GS4, GS9,
GS12, GS25, GS52, M6,
M16, MS2, MS4, MS7,
MS10, MS12, MS13,
MS21, MS22, MS23,
MS25, MS28, MS29,
NT2, NT3, NT8, NT9,
NT12, NT13, NT23,
NT26, NT29, NT37,
NT38, NT40, NT41,
NT44, NT45, NT50,
NT55, NT56, NT74,
NT75, NT80, NT82,

NT83, NT87, NT88,
NT89, NT90, NT91,
NT96, NT97, R5, SN3,
SN9, VE25, VE28,
VE30, VE39, VE46,
WS26, WS33
Communications (CM1–
CM15): CG54, DH22,
EE5, EE10, GS5, GS7,
GS15, GS17, GS31, I23,
NT64, T8, T10, T14,
T34, VE27, WS12,
WS34
Computers (CP1–CP17):
CG30, CG40, D18, MS5

Discrimination (D1–D25):
B1, CG28, CG35, CP14,
DH1, FW14, GS56, L2,
L3, L5, L7, L9, L11,
L12, L13, L14, MS6,
MS40, NT39, NT43,
NT57, NT71, NT76,
PT1, T17, VE11, VE18,
WS11, WS37
**Displaced homemakers/Reen-
try women** (DH1–
DH27): B5, B31, B32,

Beverly A. Stitt is an associate professor of information systems in the College of Technical Careers and the coordinator of Women's Studies at Southern Illinois University at Carbondale. She is the author of *Building Gender Fairness in Schools*, a preservice and an in-service teacher education textbook. Her gender issue research has appeared in numerous journals, training manuals, and conference proceedings. She is a frequent consultant to business, industry, and government agencies.